THE HAPPY LEADER

A Modern Playbook for Energy, Empathy, and Everyday Leadership

By

Melissa Maloney

ACKNOWLEDGMENT

Writing this book has been a journey shaped by countless conversations, challenges, and connections throughout my career. While leadership is often framed as a solitary pursuit, the truth is that none of us lead or grow alone.

I'm grateful to those who offered their time and feedback, reading this in advance, whose careful eyes and thoughtful input helped refine these ideas and ensure clarity in every chapter.

My deepest gratitude goes to Jennifer Slay, my partner in crime, whose collaboration and unwavering support have been instrumental in bringing these ideas to life. To my children, Freedom and Alexis, thank you for understanding the late nights and early mornings, and for (mostly) forgiving me when work demanded more than I wanted to give. Your grace has meant everything. I know often you were "managed" just like my team, and I am grateful for your ability to see (some) of the value in it now that you are leading in your own careers.

I've been fortunate to have extraordinary mentors who exemplified the principles in this book. Kathy Kaye guided me through my early career with patience and wisdom. Jane Riddell has consistently demonstrated what it means to be a Level 5 leader, humble, driven, and deeply committed to others' success. Gord Hart became one of my greatest allies and mentors, showing me what true advocacy looks like and inspiring me to believe anything is possible. And Neil James has been both an incredible mentor and friend, offering guidance that has shaped not just my career, but who I am as a leader, and the courage to jump when I didn't think I could.

To my Women's League friends: thank you for creating a space where we can challenge each other, celebrate our wins, and hold each other accountable to becoming better leaders. That kind of community is rare and precious.

My besties Lisa, Melissa, and Julie have listened to countless hours of frustrations, crazy ideas, and tears on the hardest days. My sister Nicole has been there in a way only she can, with the kind of support that doesn't need explanation. Thank you all for anchoring me.

And to my biggest cheerleader, who knows exactly who they are: thank you for the constant reminder that changing the world takes time, and for believing in me, especially when I doubt myself and my value.

To everyone who has invested in my growth, challenged my thinking, and supported this journey, this book exists because of you.

DEDICATION

To every leader who shaped me through both their wisdom and their missteps, and to the many team members who trusted me with their growth and, in doing so, allowed me to become my best self.

TALE OF CONTENTS

Introduction For the Leader Who Wants to Get It Right

If you've picked up this book, there's a good chance you're a leader who wants to make things better, for yourself, your team, or maybe both. Maybe you are a new leader, maybe you are an exhausted leader, maybe you have said to yourself, "There has to be a better way..." You might not always feel like you have it figured out, but you care deeply about doing the right thing.

That's where *The Happy Leader* begins.

I wrote this book for people like us, people who believe leadership is about humans, not hierarchies. For people who are trying to balance results and relationships, who want to lead with empathy but still drive performance. For people who sometimes feel like they're spinning. I've been there too.

When life or leadership felt heavy, books have always been the thing that helped me stop the spinning. The right words at the right moment can quiet the noise, create clarity, and remind us that forward is still forward, even when we can't see the whole path.

That's what I hope this book does for you.

Why This Book Is Different

You won't find endless theory here. You won't find complicated frameworks or leadership clichés.

The Happy Leader was intentionally written to be clear, conversational, and actionable.

Each chapter is short by design, something you can read between meetings or at the end of a long day, when you need to reset and refocus.

Every section ends with reflection questions because leadership doesn't grow from reading alone; it grows from action. Use these questions to pause, to ground yourself, or to bring your team into the conversation.

If something in these pages helps you breathe a little easier, lead a little calmer, or reconnect with why you started doing this work in the first place, that is all I want for you.

Simplify. Reflect. Move Forward.

Leadership can get complicated. We make plans and policies and frameworks and forget that people are at the center of it all, including us. This book is about simplifying where we can, so we have the energy to focus where it matters most. It's about reconnecting to purpose, building trust, and remembering that progress doesn't require perfection.

Like every talk I give, every session I facilitate, and every client I coach, my goal with this book is simple: to help you see that you can figure it out.

Because leadership isn't about having all the answers; it's about taking the next step, knowing it may not even be the right one, learning as you go, and helping others do the same.

So take what you need from this book. A single line, a chapter, or even one reflection question might be the thing that helps you stop the spinning and move forward with intention.

Welcome to *The Happy Leader.*

Let's figure it out together.

Writer's Note

You'll notice that Part One of this book is longer than the rest. That's intentional.

Becoming a happy leader starts with you and self-awareness, the part of leadership that takes the most time, practice, and reflection. Each section that follows gets a little shorter, not because there's less to learn, but because clarity makes things simpler. Once you understand yourself, leading others and building culture becomes more intuitive. These chapters are designed to feel lighter, faster, and more actionable as you go, a reflection of what happens when leadership moves from learning to living.

Part One
Be Your Best Self

Leading from the Inside Out

Every leadership journey begins here, not with a title, but with a decision. The decision to lead yourself first. Before you can build trust, inspire others, or create impact, you have to know who you are and how you show up.

This part is about clarity and energy, understanding your mindset, your emotions, and the patterns that shape your choices. You'll see Alex wrestle with the fog of exhaustion and rediscover her direction. You'll find tools to manage your energy, calm the noise, and build a foundation of emotional intelligence that lasts.

Because before you can help others live happy, you have to learn how to lead yourself there.

Prologue
The Breaking Point

This is the story of Alex, and her journey from being burnt out and overwhelmed as a manager to becoming productive and efficient as she learns the Happy Leader Method alongside you!

Alex Carter hated Mondays. As Sales and Marketing Manager, it was always the start of another week that would turn to chaos.

But this Monday was different.

The sales dashboard glared back from her laptop, numbers down for the third quarter in a row. Another email sat unopened in her inbox that she was sure was a resignation. The team group chat was silent except for one lonely meme meant to motivate.

And in less than ten minutes, she was due in her VP's office.

She sat with her head in her hands, trying to remember the last time she felt like she was winning. She couldn't. The team was tired. Both finding new customers and keeping customers seemed to be dragging. Every day, she felt like her job became more about putting out fires and solving crises, trying to keep everything afloat instead of doing the actual work.

The meeting was mercifully short. The VP's tone was cool, almost clinical:

"You've got 90 days to turn this around. If we don't see improvement... we'll have to make changes. I'm getting a ton of pressure from above; they say I need to look at leadership as the first step in those changes."

By the time Alex left, the hallway felt smaller, the air heavier. Ninety days might as well have been ninety minutes, given how lost she felt.

She slumped into her chair and stared at the wall. Then, as if the universe had a sense of timing, her phone buzzed.

Mel: *Coffee today? My treat. We haven't caught up in months.*

Alex exhaled, somewhere between a laugh and a sigh. Mel had been a mentor years ago, someone who always seemed to see around corners. Maybe coffee was exactly what she needed. Or maybe it was one more meeting she didn't have time for.

Still... something in Mel's message felt like the extra breath she needed.

Chapter 1
The Monday That Changed Everything

The coffee shop was warm and loud, a welcome contrast to the sterile quiet of the office. Mel was already there, waving from a corner table, two lattes sitting on the table.

"Rough morning?" Mel asked.

"That obvious?" Alex collapsed into the chair. "I've got a team that's running on fumes, customers who've lost patience, and a boss with a ninety-day countdown over my head."

Alex started to explain what was going on at work and all the fires she had been putting out. She was going so fast she didn't even stop to take a breath. Mel listened without interrupting, just nodding slowly.

"So... how are you doing?" Mel finally asked.

"I just told you..."

"No," Mel cut in. "That's how your team is doing, and how everything at work is doing. How are *you*?"

Alex hesitated. "I'm tired. I don't remember the last time I felt ahead. Everything is urgent. Everyone is frustrated. And I feel like I am losing control. It's like the world is spinning faster and faster, and I just can't keep up."

Mel leaned back, smiling just enough to be infuriating. "You can't lead them if you're running on empty. If you don't have energy to give, how can you possibly give them the energy they need?"

"I don't have the luxury of taking a break, Mel. This is sink or swim."

"Exactly," Mel said. "And right now, you're paddling with one arm tied behind your back. You want the team to win? You've got to start with *you*."

Alex frowned. "I thought leadership was about putting the team first."

"It is," Mel replied. "But if you're exhausted, distracted, and out of alignment, you're handing them the same energy you're complaining about. People don't wake up in the morning saying, 'I'm going to fail today.' But they'll fail if they don't have the right environment. And you're the one who sets it."

Alex sat back, the words landing heavier than she expected.

Mel leaned forward. "You've got ninety days, right?"

Alex nodded.

"Perfect. Give me ninety days, too. We'll figure it out together."

Something in the way Mel said "we'll figure it out" felt like more than a challenge. It felt like a promise.

Chapter 2
People Don't Wake Up Wanting to Fail

When things go wrong, leaders often go hunting for the problem "out there," the market, the customers, the economy, the team. It is easy to always look to external factors as to why challenges are happening, and if you look hard enough, I promise you will find the proof you need to validate it. The reality is that the long-term success of a company more often happens due to internal factors such as leadership, organizational efficiencies, and innovation.

And since you are reading this book, let's start with the thing we can control the most, YOU!

The truth is, your people take their cues from you. And even if they don't, if you are feeling stressed out, overwhelmed, and like you are running on empty trying to get everything done, this is not what you want your work life to feel like for the next 30 years!

That's why Mel told Alex to start with herself. And that's why the first step of The Happy Leader Method is "Be Your Best Self."

Here's the truth:

"People don't wake up in the morning saying, 'I'm going to fail today.'" Or "I'm going to suck today." And they most definitely don't say, "I want to piss off my boss today."

They might wake up tired. They might wake up worried about their mortgage. They might wake up unsure of what's expected of them. But they aren't plotting failure.

And I am guessing that is not what you think in the morning either. So if you don't think that, why would your people?

When people fail, it's usually because the environment doesn't set them up to succeed, and that environment starts with you.

The Happy Leader Method has four core pillars:

1. Be Your Best Self
2. Build Great Relationships
3. Everybody Wins
4. Help Others Live Happy

Most people-related challenges you face as a leader will fit into one of these pillars.

And here's the trap most leaders fall into: they jump to helping others without first doing the work of *Be Your Best Self*.

The Mirror Effect:

If your team mirrored your energy, mindset, and behaviours for the next 30 days, would that be good or bad? If they went home at the end of the day feeling how you are feeling, would you be excited about that?

For Alex, the answer was clear, and not in a good way.

Your First 90-Day Shift:

Start each day by checking your energy before your email. Self-awareness is always the first step. Assume your people want to win. If you start from this position, it will always lead to a better outcome. Lead yourself first, then lead your team.

A good reflection question each day, as we start on this journey together, is to ask yourself:

If my team mirrored me today, what would change in their performance, energy, and attitude?

Chapter 3
Running on Empty

Alex sat at her desk long after everyone else had left.

The office was silent except for the hum of the HVAC and the pings of incoming emails, texts, and notifications. Each ping brought a small jolt of anxiety, a reminder of yet another thing she hadn't done.

She re-read the same sentence for the third time. Her brain felt like it was wading through wet cement. She'd pick up her phone, scroll aimlessly, lose track of time, then feel that familiar wave of guilt crash over her. It was a cycle that seemed impossible to break.

It wasn't just today.

This was every day.

Wake up tired. Rush through the day. Collapse at night. Repeat.

Earlier that week, one of her top performers had asked, "Are you okay?"

She'd laughed it off with a quick, "Just busy." But the truth was, she wasn't okay.

Her phone buzzed.

Mel: *Tomorrow. Coffee. No excuses.*

The next morning, Alex slid into the booth across from Mel. Before she could say anything, Mel leaned in.

"How are you doing?"

Alex exhaled. "You know the answer. And that's why we're here. I know you said we'll figure it out, but honestly, I can't see the solution right now... and that scares me."

Mel nodded. "Then we start with the one thing you can control: your energy. Before you can lead anyone else, you have to be your own Chief Energy Officer."

Alex raised an eyebrow. "Sounds... corporate."

"It's not," Mel said with a small smile. "It's survival. You know the saying: you can't pour from an empty cup, and right now, yours is bone-dry. So let's talk about filling it."

Mel pulled a napkin from the dispenser and drew four boxes.

"These are the Four Energy Systems," she said, sketching quick titles: *Physical, Mental, Emotional, Spiritual.*

"Physical energy," she explained, "isn't about training for a marathon. It's about moving your body every ninety minutes, eating real food, hydrating well, and getting enough sleep each night, not to mention taking time to recharge and relax."

"Mental energy," she continued, "is about protecting your focus: shutting off notifications, blocking time for your best work, and prioritizing what you do best. Not what's loudest or most urgent, but what's most valuable."

"Emotional energy is about being in an environment where you feel safe and trusted. It's about keeping your mindset strong and not letting negativity set the tone."

"And spiritual energy, that's the 'why' behind what you do. The meaning. The way you give value back."

Alex studied the napkin. "So... if all four are low?"

"You're running on empty," Mel said. "And here's something Marcus Buckingham teaches: your strengths will energize you. Your weaknesses will drain you. Right now, I'd guess you're spending most of your time in drain mode."

Alex thought about her last week: constant status meetings, admin work, customer fires. Almost none of it played to her strengths.

Mel leaned forward. "Here's your homework. For one week, track everything you do, every hour. Then mark whether it energized you or drained you. And while you're at it, spot the time-wasters. You'll be amazed at how much of your day goes into things that pull you away from being your best self."

Alex smiled faintly. "Sounds... confronting."

"It is," Mel said. "But that's where the magic starts. Because once you see the pattern, you can shift it. That's when your energy starts to come back. And once your energy comes back, everything else changes, your focus, your mood, even the way your team shows up."

Alex folded the napkin and tucked it into her bag like it was a secret map.

She didn't know it yet, but in the weeks to come, that little square of paper would become the foundation for turning it all around.

Alex also didn't know it yet, but Mel planned on bringing up these four energy systems throughout their meetings.

Chapter 4
Energize

Leadership is an energy transfer.

If you show up depleted, your team will feel it. If you show up energized, they'll feed off that.

That's why the first step in *Be Your Best Self* is **Energize**.

The Four Energy Systems: Your Foundation (See Appendix 1)

1. Physical Energy

Every 90 minutes or so, your body naturally cycles through high and low energy phases. In chronobiology, this is called an ultradian rhythm, or the Basic Rest–Activity Cycle. During the high phase, you're alert, creative, and able to focus deeply. But as the cycle winds down, you start to feel distracted, restless, or mentally foggy. The temptation is to push through, grab another coffee, and power through emails, but here's the truth: when you fight your body's natural rhythms, you're swimming against the current.

I know what you're thinking: "But I don't have time to take a break essentially every 90 minutes." Here's the thing: you don't need a full break. You just need a reset.

Research shows that brief movement, even just 60 seconds, can snap you out of that low-energy slump. A short burst, standing up, stretching, walking a few steps, signals your body to re-engage. These micro-breaks have been shown to elevate energy use by 20–60% and improve focus and attention by up to 40%. That's not theory; that's science-backed performance. You can bounce on the spot, do some deep breathing, stretch, or just get 60 seconds of intentional movement.

And here's where I really want you to lean in: physical energy is more than just a body thing. It's the fastest way to reset your mind. Back in my fitness-industry days, I learned this firsthand. After a hard sales call that didn't go the way I wanted or a difficult conversation with a team member, I didn't sit at my desk and feel frustrated. I'd head for a run. Sometimes it was twenty minutes, sometimes it was a full hour, but every time, I came back clearer, calmer, and more capable of leading.

That's because movement doesn't just burn calories; it burns off mental clutter. It gives your brain space to process, to reset, to let go of the emotional weight of the moment. It's like hitting the refresh button on your day.

So here's your challenge: for the next week, start noticing your 90-minute cycle. When you hit the low point, before you reach for caffeine or sugar, and definitely before your phone, stand up. Move. Stretch. Walk to refill your water. If you can, step outside for a couple of minutes. It's not about exercise; it's about energy management. Do it consistently, and you'll notice you have more in the tank not just for you but for the people you lead.

2. Mental Energy

Protecting your focus means having uninterrupted time, turning off notifications, and scheduling your best work when you're at your sharpest. It's also about prioritizing what you do best and not scattering yourself across too many low-value tasks.

In the days before notifications, if you needed something from a colleague, you would have to walk to their desk, talk to them face-to-face, and have a complete conversation. You might plan what you needed to say, anticipate their questions, and then return to your work. Now we are more accessible than ever, but less available. Our devices keep us "on call" for anyone at any time, and the constant drip of pings, buzzes, and vibrations takes over our attention.

The science is clear: every time we are pulled off task by a notification, our brain experiences what researcher Sophie Leroy termed *attention residue*. Part of our cognitive processing stays stuck on the original task, reducing our capacity to fully engage with the new one. Studies from the American Psychological Association have shown that it can take over 20 minutes to regain full focus after an interruption. Frequent task-switching also comes with a measurable cognitive cost; research from *Harvard Business Review* reports that people can lose up to 40% of their productive time to the "switching penalty."

Those constant micro-disruptions not only slow you down, but they also deplete your mental energy. You're asking your brain to reboot dozens of times a day, leaving you mentally fatigued much earlier than you should be.

That's why one of the most powerful ways to protect your mental energy is to turn off your notifications and create intentional boundaries about where, how, and when you communicate.

But there's another layer to this: choice.

When you consciously choose how you spend your time, instead of letting other people's priorities dictate your day, you protect your mental energy like nothing else. Choice reinforces control, and control reduces stress. Even small decisions, like choosing to finish your current project before responding to a message, can signal to your brain that you are in charge of your focus. Over time, this sense of agency builds confidence, reduces mental clutter, and helps you stay aligned with your most important work.

We'll go deeper into the mechanics of scheduling in the "Prioritize" section, but for now, the key is understanding when in your day you are most naturally productive and aligning your most important work with those windows. By focusing your mental energy on your highest-value tasks at the right time and deliberately choosing where your attention goes, you maximize clarity and output without burning yourself out.

3. Emotional Energy

Emotional energy is the fuel that comes from feeling safe, trusted, and respected in your environment. It's the space where you can show up as your true self without fear of judgment, retaliation, or disrespect. When trust is high and psychological safety is present, you can focus fully on your work because your mind isn't burning energy on self-protection.

But when trust is low, the opposite happens.

Instead of simply communicating, you start managing every interaction, rehearsing your words, double-checking your tone, and analyzing how your message might be received. You think about who's in the room before you speak, carefully weigh the potential fallout of an idea, and often hold back altogether. This isn't just a mental drain; it's an emotional burden. It's the constant hum of tension that quietly drains your energy all day long.

It's like running a computer with too many programs open. Even if you're technically "working," background processes are eating up your processing power. Over time, this constant vigilance leads to fatigue, irritability, and disengagement.

Psychological safety, a term made widely known by Dr. Amy Edmondson's research at Harvard, is the belief that you can take interpersonal risks without fear of negative consequences. It's not about avoiding all conflict or disagreement; it's about creating an environment where people feel free to ask questions, admit mistakes, and offer ideas without bracing for impact.

Here's the connection to energy: when you can show up as your authentic self, you eliminate the constant "translation" layer between who you are and who you think you're allowed to be. That frees up mental bandwidth, sharpens creativity, and allows you to fully engage without the drag of censorship.

Think about the difference between working with someone you trust completely versus someone you have to "handle" carefully. With trust, your communication is straightforward, your collaboration is easy, and your focus stays on the work itself. Without it, you're splitting your attention between the task and the emotional management of the relationship, and that second part is exhausting.

Protecting your emotional energy means actively cultivating trust and safety with your team, setting boundaries that protect your values, and contributing to an environment where others feel the same. When emotional energy is high, teams can challenge each other, innovate, and navigate conflict without damaging the relationship. And for you as a leader, it means you can use your energy to drive progress instead of burning it on self-protection.

4. Spiritual Energy

Spiritual energy isn't about religion; it's about meaning. It's the energy you get from knowing that what you do matters, that your work is connected to something bigger than a task list or a paycheck.

When you're connected to your "why," the work becomes more than a job; it becomes a contribution. It's the difference between "I assemble car seats" and "I help protect children's lives every single day." The task is the same, but the energy you bring to it, and the energy you get back, changes completely.

Purpose has a multiplying effect on your energy. When you believe that what you do matters, you can push through challenges, find creative solutions, and show up on days when your physical, mental, or emotional batteries aren't at 100%. It's the invisible fuel that makes the hard work worth doing.

But here's the reality: not every job is going to hand you a purpose on a silver platter. Some roles are repetitive. Some feel far removed from the impact they create. That doesn't mean you can't find meaning, it means you might have to look beyond your job description to see it.

If your work doesn't naturally connect to your "why," you have two options:

- Find the thread: Look for how your work contributes to a larger picture. Maybe you're not designing the product, but your accuracy in data entry ensures the company delivers on time, which keeps customers happy and employees paid. Your part matters.
- Find it outside of work: Your purpose can live beyond your career. It can come from volunteering, mentoring, raising a family, supporting a cause, coaching a team, or contributing to your community. When your job doesn't fill your "purpose cup," make sure something else in your life does.

Without spiritual energy, even well-paying, comfortable jobs can feel hollow. With it, even challenging work can feel worthwhile. And as a leader, when you help your team connect to the "why," whether inside or outside of work, you're not just improving morale, you're fueling the deepest layer of their energy system.

Energy System Self-Reflection Questions

1. **Physical Energy**
    - When I hit a low-energy point, how can I prioritize a reset?
    - How often do I intentionally move during the workday (even for 60 seconds)?

- In the past month, what activities have I used to "clear my head" and restore energy after stress?

2. **Mental Energy**
   - How often do I turn off notifications or set "do not disturb" times?
   - In a typical day, how many times am I interrupted, and how quickly do I return to full focus?
   - Where am I letting other people's priorities dictate my time instead of making intentional choices?
   - When in my day am I at my sharpest, and am I protecting that time for my highest-value work?

3. **Emotional Energy**
   - Do I feel safe speaking openly and being my true self in my workplace?
   - In the last week, how often did I hold back ideas or feedback for fear of how they would be received?
   - Who in my life or workplace gives me energy, and who drains it, and why?
   - What steps could I take to increase trust and safety in my key relationships at work?

4. **Spiritual Energy**
   - How connected do I feel to the "why" behind my work?
   - If I stopped doing my job tomorrow, who or what would be impacted?
   - Does my current role give me opportunities to contribute in a way that feels meaningful to me?

- If not, what can I do outside of work to ensure I'm playing a meaningful part in the world?

The Strength-Weakness Energy Principle

Marcus Buckingham teaches that your strengths energize you and your weaknesses drain you. It's easy to mistake a strength for something you're simply good at, but that's only part of the story. A true strength leaves you feeling more alive after you've done it. You might feel challenged in the moment, but when it's over, you're energized, engaged, and ready for more.

A weakness, on the other hand, might be something you can do well, maybe even better than most, but it takes more out of you than it gives back. You finish the task feeling drained, often with a little mental resistance to starting it in the first place.

Here's an example:

- For one leader, presenting to a large group is a strength. They walk off stage buzzing with energy, ideas, and a sense of connection.
- For another, that same presentation might be a weakness. They can deliver it flawlessly, but the mental and emotional toll leaves them exhausted for the rest of the day.

The point isn't to eliminate all weakness work, that's unrealistic. Every role comes with responsibilities that might not naturally energize you. The key is increasing the percentage of your day spent in activities that give you energy.

Why does this matter for your overall energy system? Because your brain and body don't differentiate between "mentally tired" and "physically tired." Spending too much time on weakness work drains your overall energy reserves, making it harder to focus, harder to lead, and harder to stay motivated.

Think of it like a battery:

- Strength work charges the battery while you work.
- Weakness work drains the battery, even if you're "performing well."

Your job as a leader, and as your own Chief Energy Officer, is to design your day so that you're recharging as you go, not waiting until the weekend or your next vacation to recover. We will talk even more about how to use these awarenesses in the prioritize section.

Over time, this shift changes more than your schedule, it changes how you show up. When more of your time is spent in your strengths, you bring better energy, clearer thinking, and greater resilience to everything else you do.

The Time Tracking Activity (see appendix 2)

For the next week:

1. Track your time: Write down what you're doing in 30–60-minute blocks.
2. Mark each task: "E" for Energizing, "D" for Draining, "T" for Time Waster.
3. Review patterns: What percentage of your time is spent in energizing activities? What can you delegate, drop, or streamline?
4. Choose one change: Identify one small shift that will increase your energy by at least 1 percent next week.

Your Role as Chief Energy Officer

For yourself: Protect and replenish all four energy systems.

For your team: Recognize their energy patterns, encourage work in their strength zones, and create conditions for recharge.

Small shifts matter. For Alex, that meant taking a walk at lunch, turning off notifications for two hours each morning, and ending her day with one meaningful conversation. Those changes may seem small, but they were the first steps toward refilling her cup and leading with energy again.

Chapter 5
The Alignment Gap

Alex's day started with a decision, and then another, and another. By the time she'd finished her first coffee, she'd already agreed to move a meeting, respond to two client emails, approve a marketing draft, and add a last-minute one-on-one to her calendar.

None of it had been planned. None of it had been strategic.

She was saying yes to everything without thinking about what it meant for the rest of her week.

Mid-morning, she got a message from a colleague in another department: "Hey, we're putting together a cross-functional task force to explore a potential product launch. Would you be willing to join?" The presentation wouldn't happen for another six weeks, so Alex said yes without hesitation.

It was only later, when she looked at her calendar, that she realized the prep meetings would overlap with the final push on her team's biggest proposal of the quarter. If the launch didn't even get greenlit, the time investment would be for nothing.

By lunch, Alex was sitting in a meeting that had started as "urgent" but was now deep in the weeds of an internal conflict. Two people on the call were pointing fingers, rehashing old grievances that everyone else was playing into, with only one trying to mediate.

Mel's words came back to her: "You respond instead of lead. You react instead of choose."

The conversation wrapped without resolution, and Alex couldn't shake the feeling that she'd just lost an hour she'd never get back.

That afternoon, she opened an expense report that needed approval. One line item made her pause: a $200 wellness credit a team member had used for a fitness app subscription. It was a benefit the company offered, but one Alex had never personally used. She realized she'd been putting off her own health choices for months while approving them for others.

As she shut her laptop that night, Alex thought about how she'd actually spent her time: putting out fires, sitting in other people's drama, committing to things without weighing the cost, and ignoring the activities that would have fueled her energy.

Her values were rooted in growth, health, and meaningful contribution.

Her calendar told a different story.

Chapter 6
Prioritize

Alex's brain was buzzing from the overwhelm she was feeling as she put out fire after fire. She had not yet learned the power of prioritization, not in the traditional sense, but in an actionable sense! If you want to understand why your calendar feels full but your results feel thin, you have to start with one simple truth: everything you do is the result of a decision.

- What you focus on.
- What you ignore.
- Who you spend time with.
- What you say "yes" to and what you decline.

The way you make decisions doesn't just shape your calendar; it shapes your energy, your relationships, and your results.

The Volume Problem

The average adult makes about 35,000 decisions a day. That's not a typo, 35,000.

Researchers at Cornell University found that we make over 200 decisions a day about food alone. Most are unconscious, your brain's autopilot firing based on habits and environmental cues. Others are conscious, requiring effort and weighing options.

And here's the thing: we don't make decisions in a neat, linear order. We make them in the chaos of real life, while answering emails, fielding texts, thinking about dinner, and trying to remember where our keys are. Every one of those decisions, big or small, consumes energy. That's why decision fatigue is real: as the day goes on, your ability to make high-quality choices drops.

Decisions → Feelings → More Decisions

Every decision triggers a feeling:

- You say "yes" to a new client → excitement.
- You skip the gym → guilt.
- You delegate a task → relief.
- You accept a meeting you don't need → resentment.

The tricky part? These feelings are often temporary. They're short-term dopamine hits (or dips).

Neuroscience tells us dopamine isn't just about pleasure, it's about anticipation. Sometimes the thought of doing something feels better than the reality. And sometimes, the short-term high of saying "yes" (acceptance, validation, belonging) leads to a long-term drain (overcommitment, burnout).

This is normal. You're not "bad" at decision-making because you fall into this loop, you're human. The key is self-awareness. Start noticing when you're making a decision for the immediate feeling instead of the lasting value.

One way to catch yourself in the moment is to use this simple trick: ask yourself, "If I had to do this tomorrow, would I still say yes?" If the answer is no, you probably shouldn't say yes now.

Return on Time (ROT)

This is where we start filtering decisions differently.

ROT is about asking:

- Will this choice duplicate my time? (e.g., wellness, learning, systems, things that give back more time or energy in the future.)
- Will this choice minimize my time? (e.g., gossip, rework, tasks that drain energy and focus without creating progress.)

A tool you could consider is Stephen Covey's time management matrix. If you keep this in mind when making decisions or analyzing how your time is spent, it can help you identify opportunities for more "ROT."

Stephen Covey's time management matrix breaks work into four categories (see appendix 3).

Quadrant 1: Urgent + Important Crises, deadlines, problems that can't wait.	**Quadrant 2:** Not Urgent + Important Relationship-building, planning, skill development, prevention, strategy.
Quadrant 3: Urgent + Not Important Interruptions, some emails, most meetings, other people's "emergencies."	**Quadrant 4:** Not Urgent + Not Important Timewasters, mindless scrolling, busywork.

High-performing leaders prioritize Quadrant 2, the important-but-not-urgent work that moves the needle long-term. "People problems" tend to be some of our greatest time-wasters and energy drains, especially when we are firefighting problems that are presented as urgent but aren't. They are usually urgent to the person presenting them, but not to the business. This is a fine line for an engaged and empathetic leader, who can easily be pulled into non-priority distractions. Quadrant 3, on the other hand, is where much people-related false urgency lives. This is also where the Drama Triangle, described by Jim Dethmer and the Conscious Leadership Group, often takes over.

In the Drama Triangle, people unconsciously fall into one of three roles:

- **Victim** – "This is happening to me."
- **Persecutor** – "This is your fault."
- **Rescuer** – "I'll fix this for you."

When you step into any of these roles as a leader, even with good intentions, you often end up in reactive, low-ROT situations. Drama Triangle conversations feel urgent in the moment, but they rarely produce progress. Instead, they create a cycle of emotional firefighting: managing stories, egos, and conflicts that could be better resolved with clarity, accountability, and healthy boundaries.

The leadership takeaway: It's not that "people problems" don't matter, they do. But if you spend most of your "people time" in Quadrant 3 drama rather than Quadrant 2 relationship-building, trust, and skill development, you're investing leadership energy where it can't generate a return.

As we continue to align your priorities to build on your "Be Your Best Self" foundation, let's look at values.

Values as Your Compass

When your time, money, and attention are out of alignment with your values, you often feel it as guilt, frustration, or even resentment.

And this connects directly to the **4 Energy Systems**:

- **Physical Energy:** If you value health but your schedule leaves no room to recharge, your physical battery drains.
- **Emotional Energy:** If you value honesty but spend time in political games or drama, your emotional battery drains.
- **Mental Energy:** If you value creativity but your work is 80% administrative, your mental battery drains.
- **Spiritual Energy:** If you value purpose but your role feels misaligned, your spiritual battery drains.

This misalignment can show up as chronic frustration without you even realizing why.

I've seen people become managers only to realize that people leadership isn't their passion.

I've seen entrepreneurs discover they actually value the security of a steady paycheck more than the autonomy of running a business.

Self-awareness here is key, and honesty with yourself matters more than climbing the next rung of the ladder. You don't need to keep going "up" if "up" takes you further from alignment. Ensuring you connect your prioritization to your values and your decision-making is a critical leadership link. Your decision-making rhythm sets the tone for your team. If you're reactive, they'll be reactive. If you're chasing short-term dopamine instead of long-term value, they'll learn to prioritize urgency over importance.

Modelling ROT thinking, quadrant prioritization, and values alignment doesn't just make you more effective, it teaches your team how to protect their time, too.

Your team will focus on what you focus on, so getting yourself tuned up first matters! The real magic happens when these priorities start to share your calendar, that is where we are heading next.

Reflection Questions:

1. Where am I saying "yes" for the short-term feeling instead of the long-term value?
2. How often am I operating in Quadrant 2, and what can I shift to spend more time there?
3. Which relationships or conversations give me high ROT? Which minimize it?
4. If my time and money fully reflected my values, what would change starting tomorrow?
5. Where might my role or goals be out of alignment with my natural strengths and energy systems?

Chapter 7
Optimize

Alex stirred her coffee. "Honestly, I feel like I'm getting a little better at spotting where my time is going... Since putting some decision filters in play, I am noticing fewer yesses that I regret, but I still run out of gas halfway through the week."

Mel tilted her head. "Tell me, how do you plan your week right now?"

Alex hesitated. "Uh... I don't. I mean, I check my calendar and... I try to fit work around whatever meetings I already have."

Mel raised an eyebrow. "So you're building your week around other people's priorities, not your own?"

Alex grimaced. "When you put it like that..."

"That's the default for most leaders," Mel said. "We let the meetings dictate the work instead of the other way around. But here's the thing: if you don't start your week with your priorities, your people, and your values in place, everything else will fill the space."

She took a pen and started sketching on her napkin again. "Here's how I do it:

1. I block my Quadrant 2 focus time first: strategic work, planning, creating.
2. Then I schedule my people time: one-on-ones, relationship-building, coaching.
3. Then I lock in my personal priorities: workouts, family time, and the things that fuel me outside work.

Each of these three is critical for me to feel like I am spending my time on the right things. Only after that do I fit in the rest. That way, I'm making conscious decisions about what I can and can't take on."

Alex leaned forward. "So if something comes up, you already know what has to shift to make room for it?"

"Exactly," Mel said. "It slows the decision-making loop. Instead of saying yes on autopilot, I can look at my week and ask, 'Do I want this more than what I've already committed to?'"

Alex thought about her last few weeks, the number of "sure, I can do that" replies she'd fired off without a second thought, only to regret them later when she was buried in work and skipping her morning runs.

Mel continued, "This is where energy blocking comes in. Remember what we talked about when we were chatting about energy? Those 90–120 minute high-energy cycles? You use those to power your strengths. And you schedule your day so the tough, draining stuff is buffered between those strengths, what I call the Sandwich Effect. It's not just about getting more done. It's about leaving the office with energy left for your life."

Alex nodded slowly. "So the calendar becomes more than a to-do list... It becomes the way I lead myself."

Mel smiled. "Exactly. And when you lead yourself intentionally, you model that for your team."

Chapter 8
Optimize

Back in the Energize section, we learned that your energy is not constant throughout the day. You have peaks and valleys, natural 90–120-minute focus cycles that influence how well you think, decide, and create. You also discovered your four energy systems: physical, emotional, mental, and spiritual, and how they work together to power your performance. Now, we're going to put that science to work in your calendar. We are going to move from energy awareness to energy application.

Knowing your energy patterns is step one. But leaders don't just know; they apply. Optimizing means arranging your work and life so you're doing the right things at the right times, protecting your best energy for your most important priorities.

The Sandwich Effect

The Sandwich Effect works because it builds momentum and manages your energy at the same time. This is where the energy systems we explored earlier become practical scheduling tools. When you start your day with a strength-based, energizing activity, you set a positive tone. You create a small but powerful win before the day has a chance to pull you in different directions. That early momentum carries into the next task, even if it's something harder or more draining. That early win gives you an extra hit of energy and can help you get some of the biggest, most important things checked off early.

And here's the part most people miss: you don't have to limit the Sandwich Effect to just the start and end of your day. You can "sandwich" multiple times throughout your schedule. If you know a particular meeting or project will be uphill work, plan to buffer it with two downhill stretches, something energizing before and after. This way, you're never stacking energy drains back-to-back, which is one of the fastest paths to burnout.

Daniel Pink's research in *When* shows that task timing can make or break performance. Teresa Amabile's Progress Principle found that making progress in meaningful work fuels motivation, creativity, and satisfaction.

Think of it like an athlete pacing themselves through a game. They know when to push, when to recover, and how to set up for the next play. The Sandwich Effect allows you to do the same during your workday. Instead of feeling like you're slogging uphill all day, you're creating intentional rhythms, moments of flow that give you the strength to climb, recover, and climb again. It's not about avoiding the hard work; it's about approaching it with enough fuel in the tank to enjoy the ride.

One thing I also need to add here is to touch on sales calls, even the best salespeople often struggle to prioritize these calls. We can combine both the Sandwich Effect and the concepts behind spiritual energy here. These are HIGH-VALUE tasks that can also sometimes be an energy drain (rejection is no one's strength), so I do suggest scheduling these early in the day so you prioritize them, even if they are a draining activity. Why? Because somehow other things will always try to take priority over those calls, but the ultimate adrenaline rush of the sale will always outweigh the energy loss of fitting those calls in early!

Energy Blocking

Energy blocking takes everything you learned in the Energize section and puts it into motion. Instead of asking, "What will I do at 10:00?" you ask, "When is my energy at its peak, and how can I protect that time for my most important work?"

Your brain and body run on natural cycles of high focus followed by recovery dips. When you match your most valuable, high-energy work to those peaks, you get more done in less time without feeling drained. That means protecting your best focus window for strategy, creative work, or solving complex problems... and saving routine tasks or low-stakes meetings for your dips.

The beauty of energy blocking is its flexibility. You can design your day around these cycles, no matter what your role. It's not rigid. If something urgent comes up, you can shift, but you're shifting with awareness, knowing what you're giving up and when you'll get back to it. Over time, this awareness becomes second nature, and your calendar starts working for you instead of against you.

Scheduled Strategy

The concept of Big Rocks comes from Stephen Covey, who used a simple but powerful analogy: imagine filling a jar with rocks, pebbles, and sand. If you start with the sand (small, low-priority tasks), you won't have room for the rocks (the most important things). But if you put the big rocks in first, the pebbles and sand can fill the spaces around them.

Your Big Rocks might include:

- **Strategic priorities** – long-term projects, innovation, planning.
- **People priorities** – one-on-ones, mentoring, relationship building.
- **Personal priorities** – health, family time, rest, and hobbies.

Scheduled strategy means placing those rocks into your calendar first and doing it intentionally in your peak energy windows. Everything else fits around them. When new requests come in, you can clearly see what you'd have to move to say yes. That pause in itself is powerful. It slows down the decision-making loop, helping you respond consciously instead of reactively.

Intentional Leadership

Leaders who plan their weeks around energy and priorities don't just work smarter, they lead better. McKinsey found that high-performing executives spend 50% more time on long-term strategic priorities than their peers. A Stanford study showed that leaders who schedule values-based priorities see a 23% higher engagement score from their teams.

And here's the truth: leadership does not require 100-hour workweeks. The problem isn't always the number of hours; it's how those hours are used. Studies suggest that as much as 20–30% of the average workweek is lost to low-value tasks, avoidable interruptions, and unproductive meetings. That's one to two full days every week.

Intentional leadership is about creating separation, being fully present at work and fully present at home, by designing your time and energy with purpose. You don't have to choose between a successful career and a fulfilling personal life. You can have both when you stop defaulting to urgency and start designing for impact.

We also need to remember that life happens in "moments in time." There will always be moments when work may need to take a higher priority than family, and moments when family must take priority over work. When we lead with intentionality, we prepare for those moments, instead of being overwhelmed by them because we can't afford to give up either one when we suddenly really need to.

Putting It Together

Optimization is the "how" behind Energize. We've explored what it means to Be Your Best Self, showing up as the leader you want to be. You've learned how to maximize your energy, identified what's most important to you, and developed strategies for creating the time and space to lead.

And now comes the shift. Once you've built that foundation for yourself, you're ready to bring other people into the mix. Great leadership starts with self-leadership, managing your own time, energy, and priorities so you can show up fully for others.

From here, we'll move into how to build great relationships with your team, because once you have the foundation of self, you are in a position to give some of that extra energy to others. When you know how to lead yourself well, you have the capacity and credibility to lead others even better.

Reflection & Action: Optimize / Part 1

1. **Map Your Energy Sandwich**

    - Take a blank sheet or digital calendar and map out one day.
    - Mark when your energy peaks and dips typically occur (think back to the Energize section).
    - Identify at least one "uphill" (draining) task you have tomorrow or this week.
    - Use the Sandwich Effect: schedule an energizing, strength-based task before and after that uphill work.

2. **Create Your Energy Blocks**

    - Pick one high-energy block each day this week and dedicate it to a high-priority task.
    - Protect that time, no meetings, no emails, no interruptions.

3. **Schedule Your Big Rocks**

    - Write down your three most important "Big Rocks" for the next week (strategic, people, personal).
    - Put them into your calendar first, before you schedule anything else.

4. **Conscious Yes/No**

    - This week, when someone asks you to take on something new, pause and check your calendar.
    - Ask yourself: If I had to do this tomorrow, would I still say yes?
    - Only commit if it aligns with your priorities and energy.

5. **Self-Check on Intentional Leadership**

At the end of the week, review your calendar:

- How much time did you spend in Quadrant 2 (important but not urgent)?
- Did your schedule reflect both your leadership role and your life priorities?
- Where can you shift next week to create more impact with less burnout?

Part Two
Build Great Relationships

The Foundation of Trust and Team

No leader succeeds alone. The real magic of leadership happens in relationships, the spaces between people where trust, care, and accountability live.

In this part, Alex learns how to create a culture of openness and honesty. You'll explore what it means to build trust through consistency, communicate with transparency, and hold others accountable with kindness. Leadership isn't about control. It's about connection. And great relationships are what make high-performing teams, and happy workplaces possible.

Chapter 9
The Leadership Gap

Alex closed her laptop and leaned back in her chair.

The past few weeks had been different.

Not perfect. Not without challenges. But different.

She was starting to feel the fog lift. Her days had a rhythm now, bursts of focus when her energy was high, followed by recovery periods that left her sharper, not drained.

She'd learned to pause before saying "yes," to weigh decisions against her values, and to design her calendar with intention.

For the first time in months, she ended most workdays with something left in the tank.

And that's when she noticed something she couldn't ignore.

While she'd been working on herself, her team hadn't changed much. The same tensions simmered in meetings. The same few voices dominated the conversation. And the same deadlines still seemed to creep up faster than they should.

Self-leadership had given her stability, but stability alone wouldn't move the team forward.

If she wanted a culture where people could do their best work, she needed to shift her focus. It was time to look beyond her own habits and start shaping the environment around her.

Now that Alex had steadied her own footing, it was time to focus on those around her, to build the kind of trust, clarity, and connection that turns a group of individuals into a team.

Alex slid into the corner booth at the café, already smiling. "Before you ask, yes, I'm drinking water," she told Mel, raising her glass.

Mel grinned. "You're full of surprises."

"I've been doing it," Alex said. "The Be Your Best Self stuff, energizing in the mornings, blocking my high-energy tasks, using that 'sandwich effect' you taught me. I'm not as foggy. I actually have something left in the tank when I get home."

"That's great news," Mel said. "What's shifted at work?"

Alex hesitated. "That's the thing... I feel sharper, but the team's still flat. I've got more clarity personally, but it's not translating to them. I feel like I'm running at one speed, and they're just... coasting."

Mel stirred her coffee. "So, what kind of team do you want to lead?"

Alex blinked. "I mean... a good one?"

Mel tilted her head. "That's not a vision. If I could wave a magic wand and it teleported us six months from now, we watch your team, and it is exactly how you want it to be, how would it feel? What would we see? Hear? Sense?"

Alex sat back. She hadn't really thought about that. "I'd want it to feel alive. Like people actually enjoy being there. Where everyone's pulling in the same direction. No silos, no politics. And people would speak up, share ideas, help each other out without being asked. People would be winning."

Mel nodded. "And how would they describe you as their leader?"

"I'd want them to say I've got their back. That I want them to win. That I care about them as people, not just producers."

Mel smiled. “So that’s your culture blueprint: energy, unity, openness, support, and care. Now, here’s the thing, culture doesn’t happen because we hope for it. If you don’t design it, it designs itself. And it usually defaults to comfort, not performance.”

Alex laughed softly. “I think I’ve been letting it design itself.”

“Most leaders do,” Mel said. “But you’ve already built the self-awareness to notice what you want. That’s step one. The next step is to align your actions with it, every meeting, every conversation, every decision.”

Alex glanced at her notebook. “Feels like a big shift.”

“It is,” Mel said. “But it’s not about overhauling everything overnight. Start small. Ask yourself before each decision: ‘Does this move us toward the culture I want?’ If the answer’s no, rethink it.”

Alex scribbled the question down, then looked up. “This is about me first, isn’t it?”

“Always,” Mel said. “The leader sets the tone. Your self-awareness, your empathy, your belief in your people, that’s the soil. We’ll get to the trust and communication tools. But first, you need to own the culture you want to grow.”

Chapter 10
Designing Your Culture

You can't outsource culture. If you don't define it, it will emerge on its own, shaped by habits, personalities, and the path of least resistance. And once it sets, it's hard to change.

When culture happens by default, you see things like celebrating wins that may have happened by accident, not because someone had the win you want others to replicate. You may end up with meetings that involve more people than necessary because "everyone has always been invited," but as you grow, that is likely not needed. Or you could end up with a pay structure that doesn't align with your values and compensates for unwanted outcomes.

The most effective leaders design culture with intention. They don't leave it to chance, and they don't assume it will "just happen" because the right people are in the room.

This is where understanding the difference between leadership and management matters.

Management is about processes, planning, organizing, and boundaries to get work done. Leadership is about people, inspiring, guiding, and creating the conditions for others to succeed. Both are essential, but without leadership, management becomes mechanical. Without management, leadership becomes vision without execution.

Culture is built at the intersection of both. The systems, processes, and structures you put in place (management) must align with the vision, trust, and values you model (leadership).

Self-Awareness: The Lens You Lead Through

Self-awareness is the leadership lever that moves everything else. It's not just knowing your strengths and weaknesses; it's understanding how your energy, tone, and presence move through your team.

When you leave gaps in communication or clarity, your team will fill them. The problem? People rarely fill gaps with neutral assumptions. They fill them with "stories," fears, worries, and memories of when things went wrong in the past. A delayed email becomes "something's wrong." A lack of feedback becomes "they must not be happy with me." Over time, those stories harden into beliefs, and beliefs shape behaviour.

Self-awareness allows you to catch these gaps before they're filled with fiction. It means noticing:

- What mood you're carrying into the room.
- How your facial expressions or silence might be interpreted.
- Whether you might be assuming others "just know" your intentions.

When you're aware, you can lead on purpose, not by accident.

Empathy: The Curiosity to Understand

Empathy in culture building is more than kindness. It's a deliberate curiosity about the realities, experiences, and preferences of the people you lead.

Research from the Center for Creative Leadership shows that managers who demonstrate empathy toward direct reports are viewed as better performers by their own bosses. Empathy correlates with higher engagement, reduced turnover, and stronger collaboration. Gallup's data supports this: employees who feel their manager cares about them as a person are significantly more likely to be engaged at work.

In practice, as you build out the type of workplace culture you want to have, empathy means being curious and reflecting on things such as:

- Considering the cultural and personal backgrounds that shape how someone approaches conflict, deadlines, or collaboration.
- Recognizing that people have different work rhythms, some thrive in the morning, others hit their stride at 3 p.m.
- Adapting meeting structures so that quieter voices have space to contribute.
- Offering learning opportunities in multiple formats so different learning styles are supported.

When leaders approach their team with curiosity, "What's making this easier? What's making it harder? How do you work best?" They send a powerful message: Your way of working matters here. That's how you create a culture people want to belong to.

The Culture Blueprint (See appendix 4)

Culture isn't a poster on the wall. It's the shared set of beliefs, behaviours, and experiences your team lives every day. Designing it intentionally gives you a compass for every decision, from who you hire to how you handle conflict.

1. **Leader Identity**

    - **What it is:** The way you show up as a leader, your values, behaviours, and presence.
    - **Why it's important:** People take their cues from the top. If you're consistent, credible, and caring, you set the tone for the entire team. Care shows your people that you want them to win and that you have their back. Credibility

proves you can deliver what you say. Without both, trust erodes.

- **Questions to consider:**
- What three words do I want people to use to describe me as a leader?
- How do I demonstrate care in a way that feels authentic to me?
- Where do my actions and words need to better align?

2. Core Values in Action

- **What it is:** The non-negotiable principles that guide decisions and behaviour, turned into daily practice.
- **Why it's important:** Values create consistency. When they're just words, they're forgettable. When they're modelled and reinforced, they become the backbone of culture.
- **Questions to consider:**
- What are my team's natural values? Not the ones on the wall, but the behaviours we see lived every day at work that we want everyone to emulate.
- How do we celebrate behaviours that live out those values?
- Where have we allowed exceptions that weaken them?

3. Norms & Rituals

- **What it is:** The unspoken rules and repeated behaviours that shape the team experience, from meeting styles to how wins are celebrated.

- **Why it's important:** Norms and rituals anchor culture in tangible ways. They create predictability, belonging, and shared identity.
- **Questions to consider:**
- What regular touchpoints or traditions make our culture feel unique?
- Are our meetings structured in a way that supports the outcomes we want?
- Where have bad habits crept in that don't serve our goals?

4. Performance Systems

- **What it is:** The processes, tools, and feedback loops that enable people to do their best work.
- **Why it's important:** A high-performance culture doesn't happen by accident; it's supported by systems that remove friction, provide clarity, and recognize progress.
- **Questions to consider:**
- Are our systems making it easier or harder for people to succeed?
- Do we measure the right things, the ones that matter most?
- How do we course-correct without creating fear?

5. Success Picture & Action to Alignment

- **What it is:** A clear vision of what success looks like, paired with a roadmap for getting there and staying aligned.
- **Why it's important:** People can only hit a target they can see. The Success Picture paints that target in detail, while

Action to Alignment keeps everyone moving toward it, even when things shift.

- **Questions to consider:**
- If someone new joined tomorrow, could they quickly describe what "winning" looks like here?
- Do our daily priorities reflect our big-picture goals?
- How do we check in to make sure our actions are still aligned with where we want to go?

Use your blueprint as a performance metric. A strong culture isn't just a "feel-good" factor; it's the engine that drives performance.

When culture is clear, consistent, and intentional, it becomes a self-reinforcing system:

- Leaders model the behaviours they want to see.
- Values guide decision-making without needing constant approval.
- Norms and rituals create connection and predictability.
- Systems remove barriers and amplify strengths.
- Everyone knows the picture of success and how their role contributes to it.

Without that clarity, culture drifts. You spend more time putting out fires than making progress. Decisions get stuck, accountability wavers, and energy drains away.

Think of culture as the operating system of your team. Just like software, if you design it well and keep it updated, it runs smoothly in the background, supporting every "application," from projects to problem-solving. Neglect it, and bugs start appearing. Performance slows. People disengage.

The goal isn't perfection; it's alignment. When your team's values, systems, and leadership behaviours point in the same direction, culture becomes a multiplier, amplifying everything you do.

Reflection Questions:

1. How clearly have I defined the culture I want my team to experience?
2. Where do I see gaps between the culture I want and the culture that currently exists?
3. Which of the five blueprint elements is my strongest? Which needs the most attention?
4. How often do I check for alignment between my words, actions, and systems?
5. What "stories" might my team be telling themselves because I haven't provided enough clarity?

Action Steps:

1. Map your culture blueprint. Take each of the five elements and jot down what's working well and where improvements are needed. To make it easier, consider: What do I want to do more of? What do I need to stop? What do I need to start?
2. Identify quick wins. Pick one small change in each element you can implement in the next month.

There will be more tools in future chapters that will allow you to continue to create and strategize your blueprint even further!

Chapter 11
Trust Deficit

The Monday stand-up started on time. That was new. Alex had mapped out the kind of culture she wanted, but putting it into practice had not been perfect by any means.

Alex had promised the team she'd be consistent with timing, length, and agenda. She'd even sent the agenda the night before with a quick note: "Same structure each week. If I'm late, we start without me."

"Wins first," she said. "Two lines each. Go."

They went around the circle. Jamie shared about a potential customer reopening a stalled conversation. Priya said she'd booked two discovery calls. Marco shrugged. "Nothing huge."

Alex paused. In the past, she would have filled the silence with suggestions. Instead: "What's one tiny thing you did last week that moved a new relationship forward?"

Marco thought. "Got the internal champion to agree to show our tools to their team before the team makes a final decision on procurement."

"That's not tiny," Alex said, smiling. "That's a good movement step. I'm curious, what do you think made them bring us to the table?" Marco answered, and the meeting progressed.

A few smiles flickered. It felt lighter. Small, but real.

At the end of stand-up, Alex said, "I want to chat quickly about why we're changing our pipeline review." She kept it short, so she stayed on time.

"Transparency moment," she said. "Here's the 'why': our current review format catches 'misses' too late. The new format focuses on identifying opportunities earlier. Here's what I know for sure: I'll ask the same three questions every week. Here's what I don't know: the initial questions I've come up with may not be the right ones, and we might need to tweak them. We'll check in after two weeks."

The team nodded. Priya said, "Thanks for the context!" and Marco smiled and said, "Appreciate the honesty about not knowing yet."

It wasn't huge. But it was something.

Midweek, Alex kept every one-on-one. On time. No reschedules. She closed each with the same line: "What do you need from me this week to help ensure you win the week?" Then she listened.

Jamie wanted help with her mindset around a specific client. Marco needed support with getting another department to execute on a deadline they kept missing. Priya asked for help with a proposal she had built for a new prospect that would be her largest sale yet, and she really wanted it to be right.

"Can I show you what I've got?" Priya asked, hesitant. "I'm not sure it's the right way to go."

Alex felt the impulse to fix. She swallowed it. "Show me."

They walked through the proposal together. Priya rubbed her forehead. "It just looks like every other proposal, and I feel like that shouldn't be the case."

Alex said, "That's on me. I have always taken things away at this point in the process and cleaned them up. I should have spent more time helping you understand how and why we build the proposals. I haven't given you a crisp picture of what 'good' looks like." She took a breath. "I'll get that on the to-do list, and you can poke holes in it. In the meantime, let's work through this one together this time."

Priya nodded, relief and caution both showing on her face.

Thursday's pipeline review was the test. Alex followed the new structure. Same three questions, in order:

1. "Where's your greatest risk?"
2. "What did you learn?"
3. "What's the next right step?"

Jamie leaned in. "Risk: running out of time to close Jones Company. Learning: they respond to visuals best, and these keep them engaged. Next step: storyboard the rollout, three slides. Simple but visual."

"Great," Alex said. "Need anything?"

"A designer for an hour."

"Booked."

Marco's turn. He hesitated, eyes looking around the meeting. "Risk is... I'm not sure the budget exists. Learning: finance kept asking about what happens after year-one discounted pricing. Next right step... I guess ask them?"

Alex kept her tone even. "What would make that ask safer?"

"If I knew what flexibility we have to support them as a smaller and more risk-averse business."

"Got it. Let's work through some pricing guardrails together, where you have room, where you don't, and when to escalate. That's on me for not having that clearly laid out for all of you."

The room relaxed a notch. Then came the wobble.

In the last ten minutes, a senior exec dropped into the meeting unannounced and asked for a forecast update. Alex felt the old tension, the urge to perform, to speak for the team.

She caught herself. "Happy to share the roll-up after this," she said, steady. "Right now we're in our weekly team review. We committed to this agenda. I'll send you the update by 2 p.m."

The exec paused, surprised, then said, "Okay. I look forward to it later."

After the meeting, Slack pinged.

Jamie: "Thanks for protecting the time."

Marco: "Appreciated the guardrails."

Priya: "Felt different today."

Then, another message, anonymous through the team's suggestion form: *The talk is good, but it still feels risky to say when something's off. Not sure where the line is.*

Alex stared at the words. Authenticity? Better. Consistency? Better. Transparency? Better. But risk tolerance? Still unclear.

On Friday, she sent a quick video note to the team.

"Thank you for the candor in the feedback form," she said. "I'm hearing that it still feels risky to talk openly when things are not good. That tells me we haven't defined the line between 'learning opportunity' and 'avoidance.' That's on me. Next week, I'll bring a first pass at what 'good' looks like for discovery and for weekly progress, so we're aligned on expectations. We'll tear it apart together."

She hit send, took a breath, and texted Mel: *Small wins. Still a trust gap. I think expectations are the missing piece.*

Mel replied almost immediately. *Exactly. Trust needs rails. Let's connect Monday, bring your first draft of "good."*

Alex closed her laptop. It wasn't perfect. But it was progress she could feel.

Chapter 12
Trust & Safety

Trust is the foundation of every high-performing team. Without it, collaboration becomes guarded, communication slows, and creativity stalls. With it, teams move faster, take smarter risks, and recover from setbacks more quickly.

The Edelman Trust Barometer consistently shows that trust in leadership directly impacts employee engagement and retention. In their 2024 report, 79% of employees said they were more engaged at work when they trusted their employer, and 67% said they were more willing to advocate for the organization.

On the flip side, a Harvard Business Review study found that low-trust environments create measurable costs: employees in low-trust companies reported 74% more stress, 50% lower productivity, and 13% more sick days than those in high-trust organizations.

In leadership, trust isn't a vague feeling; it's the currency you trade in. Every interaction is either a deposit or a withdrawal in the trust account you have with your team. Deposits happen when you keep commitments, show care, and act with integrity. Withdrawals happen when you're inconsistent, withhold information the team needs, or act in ways that feel self-serving.

When the account runs low, people stop taking risks, stop telling you the truth, and stop believing that your words will match your actions. When it runs high, you gain something rare: the benefit of the doubt. Your team will give you room to learn, to adjust, and to lead them through change because they believe you're on their side.

Trust is something you will need to continue to build as a leader every day, but let's look at some strategies that can support building a trusting, caring, and safe environment. Brené Brown speaks about trust as small, simple actions that show you will be there consistently.

Consistency: Safety Through Predictability

Trust begins when people can predict how you'll show up. Start the meeting when you say you will. Keep the one-on-one. Use a consistent agenda. Close the loop when someone raises a concern. These are the simple ways you can build trust and safety into the processes.

Consistency doesn't mean rigidity; it means reliability. The signal is, "You can plan around me." Over time, that calms nervous systems and invites honesty because the environment stops changing under people's feet.

The more challenging part is consistency in how you show up. It's not just about keeping meetings on time or sending updates regularly; it's about the tone of your responses, your body language, and your emotional presence. People notice whether they can predict which version of you they'll get in a given moment.

If one day you respond to bad news with curiosity and problem-solving, but the next day with visible frustration or dismissal, your team will start managing you instead of managing the work. They'll adjust their words, sugar-coat risks, or avoid raising issues altogether, not because they want to hide problems, but because they're trying to avoid unpredictable reactions.

This is where emotional intelligence becomes a leadership differentiator. Daniel Goleman's research on Emotional Intelligence highlights self-management, the ability to control impulsive feelings and behaviours, manage emotions in healthy ways, take initiative, and adapt to changing circumstances, as one of the most critical leadership skills.

Leaders with strong self-management respond instead of reacting. They create a stable emotional climate where people know they can bring both good news and bad without fear of a volatile response.

Consistency in how you show up doesn't mean never expressing disappointment or urgency. It means those expressions are proportional, respectful, and predictable. Your team should know that even if you're challenging their work, you'll do it with the same values, tone, and fairness every time. That stability becomes a trust deposit in itself, one that compounds over time.

Micro-Moves:

- Standardize a few anchor processes (stand-up agenda, pipeline questions, scheduled meeting times).
- Publish your leadership "service level": what you respond to within a day, what takes a week, and what will go to the next sprint.
- Close loops visibly: "You raised X on Tuesday; here's what we did, and here's what's next."

Transparency: Context Before Control

If consistency is about predictability in how you show up, transparency is about clarity in why you show up the way you do. Secrecy breeds speculation; transparency reduces the mental load of guessing. When people don't have enough information, they fill in the blanks with their own stories, and those stories often lean toward fear, uncertainty, or past negative experiences.

Transparency is not about flooding your team with every detail. It's about offering enough context so people understand why something is happening, not just what is happening. Simon Sinek's *Start with Why* principle applies here: before you roll out a change, explain the purpose behind it, the "why," before diving into the "what" and "how." People are far more likely to embrace a decision when they understand the motivation and meaning behind it.

True transparency also includes your emotional expression. When you share honestly how something makes you feel, whether it's concern over a slipping deadline, excitement about a new opportunity, or disappointment over a missed value, you humanize the leadership role. You model that emotions are not a weakness but a guidepost, and you give your team permission to be honest about their own reactions.

Harvard Business Review research has shown that when employees understand the reasoning behind decisions, even unpopular ones, their trust in leadership increases because transparency conveys respect. It says, "I believe you can handle the truth, and I value you enough to share it."

Micro-Moves:

- Begin major communications with *why* before you move to *what* and *how*.
- Use a "Why / What I'll Do / What I Don't Know / When We'll Revisit" framework to ensure people aren't left in the dark (see appendix 5).
- When appropriate, share your emotional perspective in a grounded way: "I'm concerned because this trend impacts our ability to deliver on our promise," or "I'm proud of how you handled that difficult situation."
- Avoid spin. Acknowledge realities even when they're not ideal; your credibility grows when you're honest about the hard parts.

Authenticity: Humanity Builds Credibility

Authenticity is the bridge between what you say and what your team experiences. People can sense when a leader's words and actions don't match, and when they do match, it builds trust at an exponential rate.

Being authentic doesn't mean oversharing personal struggles or blurring professional boundaries. It means leading in a way that reflects your true values, speaking plainly instead of hiding behind jargon, and allowing your team to see the real person behind the role. That includes acknowledging mistakes, admitting when you don't have the answer, and showing genuine appreciation without it feeling scripted.

When you lead authentically, it strengthens your consistency. If you're showing up as the real you every day, there's less risk of your team encountering "different versions" of you depending on the situation. You don't have to remember which mask you were wearing last week; the mask is gone.

Authenticity also means honouring your natural style instead of forcing yourself into a personality mould you think leadership requires. If you're an introvert, you can still be highly visible and approachable by leaning into deep one-on-one conversations, thoughtful written communication, and preparation before group settings. If you're an extrovert, you might draw energy from spontaneous interactions, storytelling, and high-energy presentations. Both are valid. Your team will trust you more when they know they're getting the real, unfiltered version of you, not a performance.

Gallup's research on employee engagement has found that employees are more engaged and committed when they believe their leaders care about them as people. Authenticity is how that care becomes visible; it's proof that your concern for your team's well-being isn't just a bullet point on a slide deck.

Micro-Moves:

- Regularly check that your decisions align with your personal and organizational values.
- Share parts of your learning process: "Here's what I'm working on as a leader" invites connection.
- Adapt your leadership style to your strengths instead of trying to copy someone else's personality.
- Let your appreciation be specific and personal: "The way you navigated that client objection showed real empathy and skill."

Psychological Safety: Permission to Learn in Public

Psychological safety isn't about making everyone comfortable all the time; it's about making it safe to be uncomfortable in the pursuit of doing great work. Harvard researcher Amy Edmondson, who coined the term, defines it as "a shared belief that the team is safe for interpersonal risk-taking."

In a psychologically safe culture, people don't just feel free to share an idea, they feel expected to. They can admit mistakes without fearing career damage, ask questions without being judged as incompetent, and challenge the status quo without being labelled "difficult."

Why it matters

The reason psychological safety keeps showing up in research is simple: without it, people hold back. When employees are worried about how they'll be judged, they don't take the risk of sharing an unconventional idea, admitting a mistake, or challenging an approach that might not be working. They stay silent, even when speaking up could save time, money, or reputation.

Edmondson first identified this link when she studied medical teams and found that the highest-performing ones actually reported more errors, not because they made more mistakes, but because they felt safe enough to admit them and fix them quickly.

Google confirmed this in their landmark Project Aristotle, a multi-year study of 180 teams. Psychological safety emerged as the single most important predictor of team success, outranking technical expertise, tenure, and even raw intelligence. Teams with high safety performed better because they could debate ideas openly, learn faster from failures, and adapt more quickly to change.

The impact is measurable. Gallup has found that employees in high-safety environments are over three times more likely to contribute innovative ideas. Turnover rates drop because people stay where they feel heard and respected. And trust builds faster when it's reinforced by the lived experience of speaking up and not being punished for it.

When you create psychological safety, you're not just fostering "niceness." You're unlocking the conditions for better decision-making, faster problem-solving, and a more engaged, resilient team. It becomes the fertile ground where trust takes root and performance thrives.

The Connection between Psychological Safety, Consistency, Transparency, and Authenticity

Consistency plays a critical role in this. When your team knows they can predict how you'll react, whether you're delivering praise, handling mistakes, or addressing difficult feedback, they feel safe to engage fully. Consistency in tone, emotional regulation, and follow-through sends the message: You can count on me to respond in ways that are fair and proportionate, even under pressure. This stability reduces anxiety and gives people the confidence to bring forward ideas and issues without rehearsing or filtering themselves.

Transparency deepens that sense of safety by replacing uncertainty with context. When leaders clearly explain the reasoning behind decisions, share relevant information openly, and are honest about both challenges and opportunities, they eliminate the guesswork that fuels fear. Starting with "why" before moving to "what" and "how" demonstrates respect for your team's intelligence and fosters a climate where people believe they have the full picture. That belief encourages them to speak up because they know they're operating on the same information as leadership.

Authenticity ties these pieces together. When you show up as your genuine self, aligned with your values, open about your learning process, and willing to admit mistakes, you humanize leadership. This makes it easier for others to take interpersonal risks because they see you modelling vulnerability and imperfection without losing credibility. Your authenticity signals that you don't expect perfection from your team either; what you value is honesty, effort, and growth.

Leaders who intentionally cultivate psychological safety aren't just improving morale; they're building the conditions for sustainable high performance. By embedding consistency, transparency, and authenticity into daily interactions, they create a culture where people can focus on the work instead of managing fear, and where the best ideas can surface and take root.

Psychological Safety in Action

Model vulnerability first

If you never admit you were wrong, don't expect others to. Share a time you made a bad call, what you learned, and how you adjusted. This isn't about self-deprecation; it's about making it safe to be a work-in-progress.

Normalize learning from failure

Replace post-mortems that focus on blame with "after-action reviews" that focus on learning:

- What did we set out to do?
- What actually happened?
- What will we keep, stop, or change next time?

Ask better questions

Avoid "Why did you do that?" which can sound accusatory. Instead, ask, "What led you to that approach?" This invites explanation instead of defensiveness.

Equalize airtime

Research shows the most successful teams have relatively equal contributions from all members. In meetings, deliberately invite quieter voices: "Alex, we haven't heard from you yet; what's your perspective?"

React with curiosity before judgment

Your initial reaction sets the tone. Even if you ultimately need to correct something, start by seeking to understand: "Walk me through your thought process."

Make it part of the system, not just the moment

Build safety cues into regular processes:

- A standing agenda item for "risks & concerns" in weekly meetings
- Anonymous feedback channels for sensitive topics
- Rotating meeting chairs so everyone experiences facilitation

Embedding it into the foundation of culture

To truly stick, psychological safety must be more than an occasional leadership behaviour; it has to be woven into how the team operates. That means:

- **Onboarding:** Introduce it as a core team value from day one. Explain what it is, what it looks like, and why it matters.
- **Recognition:** Praise not only great results but also constructive disagreement, thoughtful risk-taking, and knowledge sharing.
- **Policies & norms:** Establish clear guidelines for respectful dialogue, decision-making transparency, and conflict resolution, and hold everyone accountable to them, including leadership.
- **Measurement:** Use anonymous pulse surveys to regularly check: "Do you feel safe to speak up?" Track progress over time and respond visibly to trends.

When psychological safety becomes a cultural reflex, your team won't just "feel" safe, they'll know, through repeated experience, that speaking up is valued, respected, and expected. And when safety is part of the foundation, performance, innovation, and trust don't just improve, they accelerate.

Micro-Moves:

- Start meetings by inviting input from the quietest voices first; it sends the message that all perspectives matter.
- Model vulnerability by admitting your own mistakes and what you learned.
- Recognize effort as well as results, especially in high-risk or innovative projects.
- Replace "Why did you do that?" with "What led you to make that choice?" to remove defensiveness.

Rituals: The repeatable signals that build trust

Rituals are the small, repeatable actions that communicate your values without a single slide deck or mission statement. They're the "how we do things here" cues that, over time, shape culture more than slogans on a wall ever could.

A ritual could be as formal as a quarterly strategy review where everyone, regardless of level, can propose ideas, or as informal as starting Monday meetings with "wins of the week." The point isn't the activity itself, but the consistency and meaning behind it. When rituals are predictable and purposeful, they reinforce stability and belonging.

Research from the University of Virginia found that rituals enhance group cohesion and performance by creating shared identity and predictability. They're especially powerful during times of uncertainty because they give people something familiar to anchor to.

Micro-Moves:

- End every meeting by revisiting action items and owners; it signals follow-through.
- Celebrate milestones in consistent, values-aligned ways (e.g., handwritten notes, shout-outs in team huddles, personal check-ins).
- Create "open calendar hours" where team members can drop in with questions, and protect that time as seriously as a client meeting.
- Start project kickoffs by explicitly connecting the work to the team's larger mission and values.

Bringing it together

Trust and care aren't "soft skills"; they're hard requirements for sustainable performance. The data is clear: teams with high trust work faster, innovate more, and recover from setbacks with greater resilience. And just like a bank account, the trust you build today becomes the reserve you draw on in moments of uncertainty, challenge, or change.

As a leader, you can't demand trust; you have to earn it through consistent actions, transparent communication, authentic presence, and an environment that makes it safe to speak up and take risks. And you can't outsource care; it shows up in the way you design your rituals, the way you respond under pressure, and the way you follow through on your word.

Your culture will be built by the behaviours you repeat and the moments you choose to prioritize. Start with small, deliberate trust deposits, and over time, you'll see the compounding effect: a team that believes in you, believes in each other, and believes they can do great work together. Of course, trust alone is not enough; clarity on what success looks like and how to get there is just as critical. That's where expectations come in.

Reflection & Action, Trust & Safety

Reflect

- Where am I most predictable as a leader? Where am I least predictable?
- What decisions am I keeping opaque that would build trust if I shared the "why" and "what I don't know"?
- When was the last time I modelled a learning moment in front of my team?

Do this week

- Choose one cadence to standardize (agenda, questions, or retro) and stick to it for four weeks.
- Record a 3-minute "why/what/unknowns/when we'll review" memo for a change currently in flight.

Writer's Note: This was a big chapter because it matters so much. I could not decide how or where to split the learnings; I suggest you “dog-ear” and come back a few more times. I truly wanted to make it more concise, but couldn’t. So, you may need to take the time to “absorb” it differently than other chapters.

Chapter 13
The Fog of Uncertainty

Monday morning, Alex walked into the office and noticed the tension before anyone said a word. Jamie was typing furiously, Priya looked frustrated, and Marco was scrolling through his inbox as if he were searching for something that had vanished.

"All right, team," Alex began. "How did the follow-ups with last week's prospects go?"

Jamie stopped typing. "I thought Priya was taking the client call on Thursday."

Priya frowned. "No, I thought you were sending the email after the demo. You had the notes."

They looked at each other, then back at Alex.

Marco cleared his throat. "Well, I did send something, but I wasn't sure if I was supposed to copy the manager or just send a quick thanks. So I kept it really vague."

Alex felt her stomach sink. One client had received nothing, another got mixed signals, and a third had received a generic note that didn't even mention next steps.

"Okay," she said slowly. "Let's regroup. What about the project timeline for the rollout? Where are we on that?"

Jamie flipped open his notebook. "I'm halfway done. But I thought we had until next Friday."

Priya shook her head. "Next Friday? I had it as this Friday."

Marco leaned back. "Honestly, I was aiming for the end of the month. Nobody ever said exactly when it was due."

Silence filled the room. Alex rubbed her temple. This wasn't about talent or effort; everyone was working hard. The problem was that they were working in different directions, on different timelines, with different assumptions.

After the meeting, she sat alone, staring at her notes. *I thought I'd been clear*, she told herself. *I thought they just knew what I meant.*

But the truth was unavoidable: she hadn't defined what "follow-up" looked like, who owned which parts, or when things were due. She had left space for assumptions, and her team had filled that space with confusion.

Her phone buzzed with a text from Mel.

How's the team?

Alex typed back before she could overthink it: *They're working hard, but they're lost. I think the problem is me. I never said what "good" looked like. Or when. Or who was responsible. They're trying, but they're guessing.*

A moment later, Mel replied: *That's it. Clarity is kindness. Let's talk about how you set expectations, for their sake and yours.*

That evening, Alex and Mel spoke on the phone. Alex shared the muddled client follow-ups, the mismatched timelines, and the silence that followed when she asked about progress.

Mel listened, then said, "Alex, this isn't a performance problem. It's a clarity problem. Your team can't win a game when they don't know the rules, the roles, or the results."

Alex nodded, pacing her living room. "So where do I even start?"

"Start small," Mel said. "In your next meeting, define what 'follow-up' means. Be specific. Is it a phone call, an email, or both? When does it need to happen, same day, within 24 hours? Who owns it, and what does a completed follow-up look like?"

Alex scribbled notes. "So: define results, roles, and rules. Like the who, the what, the when, and the how."

"Exactly," Mel replied. "Once you do that, accountability isn't about catching mistakes. It's about helping them succeed. We'll dig deeper into this, but for now, remember: clarity is kindness."

Alex hung up the phone, a little embarrassed that it had taken her this long to see it, but also relieved, because for the first time, she had a path forward.

Chapter 14
The Power of Clear Expectations

Clarity is kindness. When we assume, we create space for misunderstanding. When we clarify, we create trust.

Alex's team wasn't failing because they lacked skill or motivation. They were struggling because the expectations weren't clear. It's one of the most common, and most costly, leadership gaps.

Gallup's research shows that only about half of employees know what's expected of them at work. Those who do are 2.5 times more likely to be engaged. *Harvard Business Review* has found that unclear expectations drive burnout, disengagement, and rework, often more than workload itself. When people don't know what "good" looks like, they spend energy guessing, and guessing drains energy faster than hard work ever could.

Expectations = Trust + Clarity + Accountability

I always say: "No one gets up in the morning and says, 'I'm going to fail today.'" People want to win. Our role in leadership is to help them know what winning looks like. When expectations are clear, three things happen.

1. Trust grows: defining the rules of the game

Trust grows when people know the rules of the game. Without guardrails, employees spend energy guessing and second-guessing what they're allowed to do. With clear rules, they feel safe to take action and learn.

When I was training new customer service representatives, I used to tell them: "You have permission to make mistakes up to $500." That guideline gave them the freedom to make real decisions without fear of being punished for small errors. They learned faster because they weren't paralyzed by doubt. And, ironically, the mistakes rarely came close to that limit, but the clarity of the rule gave them confidence to act.

Rules like these don't restrict trust; they build it. They say: "I believe in your ability to make choices. Here are the boundaries. Inside of them, you're empowered." We can't possibly train for every scenario, but we can provide guardrails that increase confidence and consistency.

Another way to think about this comes from the tree analogy, written by Susan Scott in her book *Fierce Conversations: Achieving Success at Work and in Life One Conversation at a Time*. Not all decisions are created equal. Some are leaves, small, everyday choices that individuals can and should make without seeking approval (low risk, high autonomy). Branch decisions are moderate-risk decisions with autonomy, where team members can make the decision but need to report in afterwards. Trunk decisions are higher-risk and require consultation or reporting before executing the decision. Then there are root decisions. Root decisions are high-stakes decisions that impact the entire organization and require leadership involvement and full consultation. (See appendix 6.)

When leaders fail to clarify which decisions are leaves, branches, trunks, or roots, teams either hesitate to act or overstep and risk consequences. But when the categories are clear, people feel trusted to make leaf-level decisions, confident to engage at the right time on both branch and trunk decisions, and safe knowing that root-level calls will be made with the right level of leadership input.

I once had a team member who delayed a simple client email for days because she wasn't sure whether it was a "leaf" she could own or a "branch" that needed my sign-off, so she waited. When we clarified together that this type of follow-up was a "leaf decision," she lit up with relief. After that, she never hesitated; she acted quickly and confidently because she knew the rules of the game.

Trust grows not when leaders hold all the power, but when they clearly delegate the right kinds of power. Defining the rules, whether through dollar limits, process guidelines, or decision trees, creates the safety net that allows people to act boldly, knowing they're still aligned.

1. **Clarity strengthens alignment: who is doing what, by when**

Clarity is what turns effort into alignment. Without it, teams end up working in different directions and at different speeds, just like Alex's team in the fog of uncertainty.

Clarity means defining who is doing what, by when. It means ensuring people walk out of meetings knowing exactly what success looks like. One simple but powerful practice is to ask your team to repeat back what they heard. It's amazing how often what you thought you said isn't what they heard. Alignment comes not from talking, but from verifying shared understanding.

Processes also play a big role here. Clear processes take the guesswork out of collaboration: who owns the task, what "done" looks like, and what the timeline is. Without this level of clarity, rework and frustration are inevitable. With it, progress feels easier, and success becomes repeatable.

2. **Accountability becomes support: alignment, not discipline**

Too often, accountability is mistaken for discipline. But accountability is not about punishment; it's about alignment. It's the check that ensures we're all moving in the same direction, by the same standards, toward the same results.

When expectations are clear from the start, accountability conversations become about support: "Here's where we're aligned, here's where we slipped, how do we realign?" Instead of catching people when they fall, accountability becomes spotting them so they can land safely and try again.

Building trust, clarity, and alignment across the employee lifecycle

These principles aren't just for projects. Opportunities to create trust, clarity, and accountability exist throughout the entire lifecycle of a team member:

- Onboarding: Don't just hand a new hire a job profile and ask them to sign it. Walk through each line and explain what it means in practice. Invite questions. This creates clarity from day one and builds trust that you want them to succeed, not trip up.
- Monthly goal setting: Move beyond what is expected and dig into how. Clarify what success looks like together. Use consistent language so you and your team member are picturing the same thing.

The goal-setting model that I like to use for accountability defines outcome, performance, and process goals as three distinct types of goals. I like this model because it essentially defines three different areas of success. Each is important, and together they help identify where gaps may be occurring.

- Process Goals: The behaviours or actions we control (e.g., "make five client follow-up calls per day").
- Performance Goals: The standards of execution (e.g., "achieve 80% client satisfaction on surveys").
- Outcome Goals: The results we want to achieve (e.g., "close $100,000 in new sales this quarter").

When we focus only on outcome goals, people don't know if they're on track until it's too late. Process goals and performance goals create checkpoints and allow teams to celebrate wins along the way. They ensure people are "controlling the controllables" and can see progress, even if outcomes take longer.

The reality is that too often people focus only on outcome goals, and there are many factors we cannot control that affect outcomes. This also creates a culture where success is defined solely by results, which can backfire in two different ways. If your organization is winning, you may be celebrating a result rather than the actions that led you there. When times get tough, your team may fall into the trap of saying, "We are doing what we did before, and it isn't working," without actually knowing why. Additionally, if you focus on outcomes and not performance, you may end up celebrating bad behaviour. I once worked with a team that was winning, but not in a way that aligned with the organization's values.

Performance conversations shouldn't be limited to annual reviews. Regular check-ins reinforce clarity, celebrate progress, and course-correct early. Recognition of both good and poor performance builds fairness and trust. With clear expectations, performance conversations stop being "bad news" meetings and become growth conversations.

Setting expectations isn't a mechanical task; it's an act of emotional intelligence. Leaders who lack emotional intelligence often fall into one of two traps: pushing hard for results without clarifying the path (which creates stress and turnover), or avoiding expectations to "stay nice" (which creates goal drift and frustration).

The sweet spot is using both emotional intelligence and high drive, balancing care with clarity. To get there, leaders need to lean on three specific emotional intelligence skills:

1. **Self-Awareness: Knowing your own assumptions**

Self-awareness is the foundation of all leadership. It means asking, *"Do I really know what I expect, or am I assuming others 'just get it'?"*

Gallup research shows that managers who think they are being clear often overestimate themselves: only 41% of employees strongly agree that their job description aligns with the actual work they do. This gap exists because leaders assume their team understands expectations that were never explicitly stated.

When a leader asks a new hire to "follow up with the client," without self-awareness, the leader assumes the new hire knows that this means an email within 24 hours, cc'ing the account manager, with a personalized next step. But the new hire sends a generic note three days later. A self-aware leader would pause to check, *"Have I actually defined what I mean by 'follow-up'?"*

2. **Empathy: Understanding how expectations land**

Empathy asks, "Am I considering how my directions land on people with different experiences, work styles, or cultural backgrounds?"

Research from the Center for Creative Leadership shows that managers who demonstrate empathy toward direct reports are rated as better performers by their bosses. Empathy improves trust and collaboration because it adapts expectations to the realities of the person receiving them.

An example of this would be a leader giving the same task to two team members: one detail-oriented, one big-picture thinker. Without empathy, the leader sets identical expectations and gets misaligned results. With empathy, the leader frames the task differently: "Here's the detailed checklist" for the first, and "Here's the big outcome and three milestones" for the second. Both deliver because expectations matched their working styles.

Our role as leaders is to understand "how people work" and align our communication style with theirs.

3. **Relationship Management: Delivering expectations in a motivating way**

Relationship management asks: "Am I delivering expectations in a way that aligns and motivates, or in a way that pressures and confuses?"

According to HBR, 70% of employee motivation is influenced by their manager. Expectations delivered as orders feel like pressure; expectations delivered as commitments feel like partnership. This is a subtle line that can deliver significantly different results.

Instead of saying, "You need to get this report done by Friday or we'll miss the deadline," a leader practising strong relationship management says, "This report is critical because it informs our client's next steps. What support do you need from me to deliver it by Friday?" The expectation is the same, but the delivery shifts it from pressure to alignment.

The EQ-Drive Matrix

Expectations are as much about how you lead as what you say. Emotional intelligence and drive are the two forces that shape a leader's approach to setting expectations. Put them together, and you get four distinct leadership styles. (See appendix 7)

Toxic High Performer Low EQ and High Drive	**Empowered and Engaged** High EQ and High Drive
Detached and Disengaged Low EQ and Low Drive	**Empathetic but Unmotivated** High EQ and Low Drive

1. Toxic High Performers (Low EQ, High Drive)

Leadership Style:

- Results-focused at the expense of people.
- "Get it done no matter what" mentality.
- Relies on pressure, fear, or micromanagement.

Employee Experience:

- Constant stress with minimal support.
- High output in the short term, but morale and trust erode.
- Engagement is shallow; burnout and turnover are high.

Imagine a team member misses a client follow-up. A Toxic High Performer responds with: "*This is unacceptable. If it happens again, there will be consequences.*" The message is clear but delivered with fear, leaving the employee anxious and unlikely to take initiative again. The expectation is technically set, but trust is destroyed in the process.

2. Empathetic but Unmotivated (High EQ, Low Drive)

Leadership Style:

- Supportive and emotionally attuned but lacks urgency.
- Conflict-avoidant and overly accommodating.

Employee Experience:

- High emotional safety but little progress.
- Relationships are strong, but results are weak.

- Employees may feel cared for but frustrated by lack of direction.

Faced with the same missed follow-up, this leader says: "*I know you've had a lot on your plate, so don't worry about it too much.*" The team member feels understood but remains unclear about what is expected moving forward. The outcome is drift, everyone feels good, but nothing changes.

3. Detached & Disengaged (Low EQ, Low Drive)

Leadership Style:

- Passive, hands-off, and non-communicative.
- Provides little feedback, recognition, or direction.

Employee Experience:

- Low morale and energy.
- Apathy and presenteeism (physically present but mentally checked out).
- Employees feel invisible and undervalued.

When the follow-up is missed, this leader shrugs: "*Things slip sometimes. Let's move on.*" The employee gets no clarity, no accountability, and no support. Over time, performance decays not because people can't perform, but because they no longer see a reason to.

4. Empowered & Engaged (High EQ, High Drive)

Leadership Style:

- Visionary, emotionally aware, and performance-driven.
- Balances results with well-being.

- Clear, consistent, and motivating.

Employee Experience:

- High engagement and trust.
- People feel supported and challenged.
- Innovation, collaboration, and retention thrive.

When the follow-up is missed, this leader says:

"Our standard is that every client gets a personalized email within 24 hours. It didn't happen this time. Let's reset: what support do you need from me to make this consistent going forward?"

The employee walks away clear on the expectation, supported in closing the gap, and motivated to succeed.

Working for a **Toxic High Performer** feels like being forced to sprint full speed on a track that keeps changing direction, no finish line in sight and no time to catch your breath.

Working for an **Empathetic but Unmotivated Leader** feels like jogging on a track where everyone keeps stopping to stretch and chat, it's comfortable, but you're not getting any closer to the goal.

Working for a **Detached & Disengaged Leader** feels like wandering around the stadium with no map, no coach, and no clear race to run, you're moving, but not toward anything meaningful.

Working for an **Empowered & Engaged Leader** feels like running a race where the path is clear, the pacing is strategic, and your coach is right beside you, guiding, encouraging, and celebrating every milestone.

The 3 R's of Clear Expectations

Mel's advice to Alex boiled down to a simple framework:

1. **Results:** What outcome are we aiming for? Define success. "A follow-up means the client receives a personalized email within 24 hours that includes clear next steps."
2. **Rules:** What boundaries or standards guide us? Define guardrails. "We copy the account manager on every client email so there's visibility."
3. **Roles:** Who is responsible for what? Define ownership. "Jamie drafts, Priya reviews for messaging, Marco sends. Everyone knows their part."

When Results, Rules, and Roles are explicit, people move faster and collaborate better. People see the race map.

Use the 3 R's as a strategy to check yourself. If something is not getting done as you expect, before reacting, ask yourself: have I defined the results, the rules, and the roles? If you can't confidently say yes, you need to start there before you move to accountability alignment. By consistently using these 3 R's and teaching your team to do the same, the team can work together to ensure there is always alignment on the 3 R's before they leave a meeting.

Moving Within the Matrix

The EQ-Drive Matrix is more than theory. It's a mirror. Ask yourself: Where would my team place me today? Where do I want them to place me tomorrow?

If you lean toward **Toxic High Performer** (Low EQ, High Drive):

- Pause before reacting. Replace judgment with curiosity.
- Regulate tone and body language so accountability doesn't feel like intimidation.
- Clarify the "why," not just the "what."

If you lean toward **Empathetic but Unmotivated** (High EQ, Low Drive):

- Set deadlines out loud and confirm understanding.
- Frame accountability as support: "I care too much to let you underperform."
- Use the 3 R's (Results, Rules, Roles).

If you lean toward **Detached & Disengaged** (Low EQ, Low Drive):

- Reconnect with your team's purpose.
- Schedule consistent check-ins.
- Offer specific recognition to re-establish value.

If you aim for **Empowered & Engaged** (High EQ, High Drive):

- Balance challenge and support.
- Clarify expectations early.
- Model vulnerability by admitting your own misses and inviting feedback.

Communication Shapes Culture

Every time you set or clarify an expectation, you're shaping culture. A vague "someone handle this" creates space for dropped balls. A clear "Marco, please send this email by Thursday using our template" creates confidence. Over time, those small signals build a culture where clarity is normal and where people trust one another to follow through.

Culture doesn't emerge from slogans; it emerges from repeated, everyday communication. Clarity, practised daily, becomes culture.

Reflection & Action: Practising Clarity

1. Think of the last project your team worked on. Could everyone articulate the results, rules, and roles the same way? If not, where did the gaps show up?
2. Ask one of your team members: "What does success look like for this?" Compare their answer to yours. If they don't match, clarity is missing.
3. In your next meeting, start by stating: "Here's the purpose, here's the outcome we're aiming for, and here's who owns what."
4. Reflect: Do I lean toward avoiding expectations to stay liked, or pushing for results without enough context? How can I move toward high EQ + high drive?

Chapter 15
The Ownership Conversation

Alex stared at the project board on her screen, her stomach sinking as she scrolled. The campaign timeline had slipped again. The draft that was supposed to be finished Friday was still incomplete on Monday morning.

She could already feel the frustration rising. This was the third time in a month that deadlines had been missed. She imagined herself walking into the team meeting and demanding answers: Why didn't anyone deliver on time? Don't you realize how this affects the whole team?

But something made her pause. She remembered her last conversation with Mel about clarity. If expectations were the rules of the game, accountability was how you kept score. Still, in the moment, her default was blame.

Later that afternoon, Alex called Mel.

"I don't get it," Alex said, pacing in her office. "I laid out the deadlines, but they missed them again. I'm so tempted to just call them out, but I know that's going to tank morale. At the same time, if I don't say anything, it feels like I'm telling them deadlines don't matter."

Mel chuckled softly. "Classic leadership dilemma. Say nothing, and you lower the standard. Say it poorly, and you crush trust. But there's a third option."

Alex sighed. "Okay, what's the third option?"

"Accountability as kindness," Mel said. "You don't avoid the conversation, but you don't weaponize it either. You frame it around alignment, not discipline. Want me to show you?"

"Yes, please," Alex replied.

Mel shifted her tone into role-play mode. "All right, imagine I'm your team member. You'd start by connecting on the why: 'This campaign matters because it sets the tone for our client relationship and impacts our credibility. When we miss, it doesn't just affect a date on the calendar; it affects how much trust the client places in us.' That connects their work to purpose."

Alex nodded, scribbling notes.

"Then you clarify the gap," Mel continued. "You'd say: 'The draft was due Friday, and it's still incomplete today. That's the gap between what we agreed on and where we are now. I want to understand what got in the way.' Notice how that's behaviour-focused, not personal. You're addressing the situation, not attacking them as individuals."

Mel leaned in. "And then you listen to understand. I like to use the four accountability quadrants to guide my coaching: Can and Will, Can and Won't, Can and Can't, and Can't and Won't. Listening carefully helps me identify which quadrant I'm addressing, and from there I can decide what kind of coaching conversation needs to happen."

She paused, then added, "Once you've listened fully, you coach to action. Ask them: 'What support do you need to meet deadlines moving forward? How do we make sure this doesn't happen again?' That turns the conversation forward. It's not about blame; it's about building capacity."

Alex sat back in her chair. "Connect, clarify, coach. That feels so different than the speech I was about to give."

Mel smiled. "Accountability is alignment. And alignment is kindness. People want to win, Alex. Your job is to help them know how to win, even when they've stumbled."

Alex closed her notebook and exhaled. For the first time, accountability didn't feel like confrontation. It felt like leadership.

Chapter 16
Accountability as Kindness

Accountability is one of the most misunderstood parts of leadership. Too often, it's equated with discipline, with pointing out mistakes, or with uncomfortable conversations people want to avoid. But at its core, accountability isn't about punishment. It's about alignment. It's about trust. And it's about helping people win.

I've said it before (and will say it again before the end of this book): no one wakes up in the morning saying, "I can't wait to fail today." When someone slips on a deadline, misses a detail, or falls short of a goal, they already know it. Most of us are our own harshest critics. Letting people sit in that knowledge alone, without support or clarity, isn't kindness; it's neglect. True accountability means stepping into those moments with care, not letting people flounder in silence, and guiding them back to alignment with the standards you've already agreed on.

Why Accountability Matters

Accountability is not an add-on to culture; it *is* the culture. It is the mechanism through which trust becomes tangible. When accountability is present, teams know that standards matter, commitments are honoured, and everyone is moving in the same direction.

Research reinforces this. Gallup found that employees who strongly agree their manager holds them accountable are 2.5 times more likely to be engaged. Yet, in another Gallup study, only 14% of employees strongly agreed that their performance reviews inspired them to improve. Why the gap? Because accountability is too often delivered poorly, as a formality, as criticism, or as a one-way lecture.

Amy Edmondson's research on psychological safety at Harvard adds another layer. Her studies showed that high-performing teams don't avoid mistakes; they surface them quickly and deal with them together. The difference is that accountability in those environments isn't about shame. It's about learning.

So, if building a culture of candor is the *what*, emotional intelligence is the *how*.

Self-Awareness: Your Relationship with Accountability

Every leader brings their own history with accountability to the table. For some, accountability was modelled as harsh correction, where being called into a boss's office meant bracing for criticism. For others, it was absent altogether, no feedback, no standards, just silence, which also creates a culture where, if any feedback is given, it must be bad.

Those experiences leave a mark. If accountability once felt like punishment, you might avoid it now, telling yourself you're being "kind," when in fact you're leaving people unclear. If accountability once meant relentless pressure, you might replicate that style, thinking it's the only way to drive results.

Both of these approaches create an "accountability is bad" feeling, and this is where stress and anxiety can breed. The best approach is consistency, where alignment does not trigger an emotional reaction and is understood as information, because everyone shares the same goal: performance.

Self-awareness is about noticing your default. Ask yourself: When I think of accountability, what feelings surface? Do I lean toward avoidance, or toward control? Your personal story with accountability shapes how you deliver it to others, and being aware of that story is the first step to changing it. Think back to where you land in the matrix we reviewed in the previous chapter; can you identify times when you aligned with different quadrants? This is a great way to begin becoming more aware of your defaults.

I learned this myself when leading a team of sales professionals. On the surface, some of them appeared to be missing tasks because they weren't motivated. But when I really listened, I discovered the real issue: they didn't know how to set boundaries with colleagues who constantly interrupted them during call times. Their "performance problem" wasn't laziness; it was a missing skill. It was easier to engage in conversation with their co-workers than it was to keep dialing. People will often choose the easy route, even when it is not the right one. Once I coached them on how to say, "I'd love to help, but I need to finish this first," their productivity changed.

As we have these conversations, we need to go in truly prepared to listen in order to understand, not just to point out gaps. These conversations are about identifying and uncovering what's really going on beneath the surface. The quadrants that Mel references in the story are an easy way to consider where your team is at. (see appendix 8)

Can and Will	Can and Won't
These are the employees we want to support and provide autonomy to. Ensure you don't forget them!	These employees need to have honest performance conversations, ensure expectations are aligned. They have the skills and need to understand the why, but if they won't perform then this isn't the place for them.

Can't and Will	Can't and Won't
These team members should be trained, provided the necessary tools and resources and provided the support they need to win. This typically is a training gap, or a safety gap- if they don't feel safe enough to ask for help.	Unfortunately, these are typically poor hires. They have been brought in for a role they can not complete, this is ok. But don't keep them too long, support a positive exit while the relationship is still strong.

The Care Perspective

Here's the truth: people know when they're not performing. They don't need you to tell them they've fallen short. What they need is your leadership to help them get back on track. Allowing someone to sit alone in underperformance isn't compassion; it's abandonment. Compassionate accountability says, "I see you, I know this isn't where you want to be, and I'm here to help you succeed." That transforms accountability from something done *to* people into something done *with* them.

But this kind of accountability doesn't happen in a vacuum. It requires an environment where people feel safe enough to admit mistakes, share obstacles, and ask for help. This is the essence of psychological safety: the belief that speaking up won't lead to punishment or embarrassment.

MIT Sloan's research shows that trust and open dialogue accelerate problem-solving. When people feel safe raising issues, leaders catch problems early, and accountability becomes collaboration, not confrontation. Without it, people stay silent, and silence is the enemy of accountability. With it, people bring issues forward earlier, own their mistakes, and work with their leaders to find solutions.

As a leader, it's your responsibility to build this safety. You do it by responding with curiosity instead of judgment, by making it clear that raising a concern is seen as a strength, not a weakness, and by consistently separating the person from the behaviour. Over time, these practices tell your team: "It's safe to be honest here. It's safe to learn. It's safe to be accountable."

When psychological safety is in place, accountability conversations stop feeling like confrontations and start feeling like opportunities. People no longer hide problems; they take ownership of them. They know they won't be shamed, but they also know the standard won't be lowered. That combination, safety plus standards, creates the conditions for a culture of ownership.

We'll explore ownership in more detail in a future chapter, but it begins here, with the leader's choice to frame accountability not as blame, but as care.

Connect–Clarify–Coach in Action

One of the simplest and most effective ways to practise accountability as kindness is through the Connect–Clarify–Coach model. It is important to note here that this conversation is an early one, not after a deadline has been missed multiple times or after multiple accountability conversations have occurred. The goal is that if these early conversations are done well, the bigger, more critical conversations that involve discipline will be less frequent and less necessary.

Connect on the Why. Begin by reminding your team member why the work matters, not just to you, but to the team, the organization, and to them personally. Connecting to purpose creates emotional buy-in. A study in *Organizational Science* found that employees who understand the "why" behind their work are significantly more resilient under pressure. When people see the bigger picture, accountability feels less like criticism and more like alignment.

Clarify the Gap. Once the purpose is clear, address the difference between where things are and where they need to be. Keep it specific and behaviour-focused: "The report was due Friday, and it's still not complete" is clear. "You're unreliable" is personal and damaging. Clarity without judgment creates psychological safety.

But clarifying isn't just about naming the gap; it's about listening deeply to understand why it happened. This is where the four accountability quadrants come in: Can and Will, Can and Won't, Can and Can't, and Can't and Won't.

If someone can do the work and will do it, the issue might be competing priorities. If they can but won't, the conversation is about motivation and values. If they can't but will, it's a training and support issue. And if they can't and won't, it may be about role fit. Listening through this lens keeps you from jumping to conclusions. It ensures you're not just reacting to the gap, but addressing the root cause so you can coach effectively.

It is important that you approach this conversation with curiosity and active listening, and that a baseline level of safety exists where someone can be honest and say, "I missed the deadline because I kept getting distracted, and that led to me not having enough focused time to work on it the way I needed to." In this response, you can hear the *will*, but they need help moving from *can't* to *can*, because the distractions are the roadblock.

Another example would be someone saying, "I have been working on this consistently, and I just can't get the numbers to work. I would rather ensure it is accurate than have it be on time and wrong." What we hear in this conversation is another example of Can't and Will. Where the previous example was about not knowing how to stay focused (more of a soft skill than a technical skill), this example is more technical: they don't have the tools or resources to complete the project correctly.

Coach to Action. Finally, move the conversation forward: "What support do you need to deliver on time next week? What's one step we can agree on right now?" This frames accountability as partnership. Instead of saying, "Don't fail again," you're saying, "I'm invested in helping you succeed." Coaching closes the loop by creating clear next steps and shared ownership of the solution. This conversation should include not just their next steps, but also your own, as commitments to them.

In practice, this model shifts accountability from confrontation to collaboration. It reframes missed expectations not as verdicts, but as opportunities to reset and strengthen alignment.

The EQ Connection

Accountability cannot be separated from emotional intelligence. Leaders who don't engage their EQ in these moments tend to fall into one of two traps: they either weaponize accountability, using it as a hammer, or they avoid it entirely to "keep the peace."

Toxic High Performers (low EQ, high drive) demand results without care. Their accountability conversations sound like ultimatums: "This can't happen again, or there will be consequences." On the surface, this leader may look decisive, but under the hood their emotional intelligence is unbalanced. They often have low impulse control (reactions come out sharp, sometimes explosive) paired with high assertiveness (a strong desire to direct and control). The message is clear, but the delivery leaves fear in its wake. Teams under this type of leader often deliver in the short term, but engagement crumbles, trust evaporates, and turnover spikes. People stop bringing up problems because they've learned that honesty is punished, not rewarded.

On the other end of the spectrum are **Empathetic but Unmotivated leaders** (high EQ, low drive). They care deeply about their people but shy away from hard conversations. Their accountability sounds like reassurance: "Don't worry about it, I know you've had a lot going on." Their subscale profile often shows high empathy (they can sense and feel others' emotions) paired with low assertiveness (they struggle to voice expectations clearly or to hold the line). In the moment, employees may feel cared for, but over time the lack of follow-through creates frustration and drift. The team feels good relationally, but results stall. Neither approach works. One creates fear; the other creates drift.

The goal is **Empowered & Engaged leadership**: high EQ and high drive, where accountability is consistent, caring, and clear. Leaders in this quadrant balance their EQ subscales. They pair empathy with assertiveness, impulse control with reality testing, and emotional expression with problem solving. They don't overuse one skill at the expense of another; they use the full spectrum of EQ to deliver accountability with both clarity and care. Consistently returning to this matrix will support you in strengthening the leadership style you are working to embody.

A Tale of Two Teams

Imagine two teams facing the same issue: a missed internal deadline.

In Team A, led by a Toxic High Performer, the meeting opens with a sharp rebuke: "This is unacceptable. Deadlines matter. If this happens again, there will be consequences." The room falls silent. No one speaks up about the obstacles that caused the delay, the unclear instructions, the bottleneck with approvals, or the overcommitment of resources. The project may get rushed to completion, but trust takes another hit. Over time, people stop offering ideas or raising risks, because they've learned that accountability feels like punishment.

In Team B, led by an Empowered & Engaged leader, the conversation sounds different: "The draft was due Friday, and it's still not complete. Let's talk about what got in the way and what support you need to get this back on track, so that we avoid ending up here again." The tone is calm, the standard is clear, and the leader listens before deciding on next steps. The team feels safe to share that they misunderstood the handoff process and that two people were duplicating work. Instead of blame, the moment becomes a learning opportunity, and they adjust the process together. Accountability here strengthens trust rather than eroding it.

Accountability in the Empowered & Engaged zone feels different. Employees don't dread feedback. They know it's coming regularly, delivered respectfully, and always connected to their growth. They may not love every accountability conversation in the moment, but they trust the intent behind it. And that trust becomes the foundation of ownership, innovation, and long-term results.

When leaders embrace accountability as kindness, everything shifts. Standards rise without fear. Trust grows without drift. And people feel both supported and challenged, the sweet spot of engagement.

Ask yourself: How do I show up in accountability conversations? Do I avoid, demand, or align? Your answer will determine not just your team's results, but your culture.

Because accountability isn't the opposite of care. Accountability *is* care. It is the highest form of respect you can give someone: the belief that they are capable of more, and that you'll walk with them until they get there.

Reflection & Action: Practising Accountability as Kindness

As you think about your own leadership, take a moment to reflect on these questions:

- When you think of accountability, what feelings come up? Do you see it as punishment, as care, or as something in between?
- How did your past experiences with accountability, either as an employee or in your personal life, shape the way you approach it today?
- Do you tend to lean toward avoiding accountability conversations to "stay kind," or toward delivering them with too much pressure? How does your team experience that?
- When was the last time you clarified the why behind a goal before holding someone to it? How did it change their response?
- Think about a recent performance gap on your team. If you had listened through the lens of the four quadrants (Can/Will, Can/Won't, Can't/Will, Can't/Won't), what would you have discovered?
- How can you use the Connect–Clarify–Coach framework in your next accountability conversation? What would each step sound like in your words?
- Which EQ subscales do you naturally lean on (empathy, assertiveness, impulse control, reality testing, etc.)? Which do you need to strengthen to bring more balance to your leadership?

Your challenge: This week, choose one accountability conversation you've been avoiding. Prepare for it using Connect–Clarify–Coach. Enter with curiosity, balance your EQ, and focus on alignment, not blame. Notice how the conversation feels different, for them and for you.

Chapter 17
The Weight of Silence

Alex could feel the tension the moment she stepped into the team room. The weekly check-in was supposed to be quick, but the air felt heavier than usual.

"Alright," she began, forcing a smile, "how's everyone doing with the rollout prep?"

Jamie glanced down at his notebook. Priya shuffled papers without looking up. Marco leaned back in his chair, arms crossed.

Silence.

Alex tried again. "Any blockers? Anything getting in the way?"

More silence.

Finally, Jamie spoke, but his voice was flat. "It's fine. We'll figure it out."

Priya nodded quickly. "Yeah, all good."

Alex frowned. She knew it wasn't all good. The timeline was slipping, and small mistakes were piling up. Last week, she had spotted three client emails that went unanswered. The data handoff had been messy, and one of the reports had errors that made the team look careless.

She took a breath. "Okay, but I'm noticing some things slipping. I want to make sure we're supporting each other."

Marco sighed, then muttered, "It's just... sometimes it feels like we're talking in circles. We don't really know what's most important. So we just... do our part and move on."

The room went quiet again. Alex felt a pang in her chest. They weren't resisting; they were holding back. It was easier for them to stay quiet than to risk saying the wrong thing.

That afternoon, Alex called Mel.

"They don't talk," Alex said. "I know there are issues, but they won't name them. I ask if things are okay, and I get silence. Or worse, I get the fake 'all good.' It's like I can see the iceberg under the water, but no one will admit it's there."

Mel didn't respond right away. Then she said softly, "Silence is heavy, isn't it?"

Alex exhaled. "It's crushing. I feel like I'm dragging everything out of them."

"Here's the thing," Mel continued. "Silence isn't a lack of communication. It's communication. It tells you people don't feel safe enough to say the truth. They're protecting themselves instead of protecting the work."

Alex sank into her chair. "So what do I do? Keep pushing? Or just let it go?"

"Neither," Mel said. "Candor is the answer. But candor only works if trust is already there. Remember: no one wakes up hoping to fail, I keep saying it for a reason. They want to win, but right now they don't know if telling you the truth will help them win, or hurt them."

Alex thought about the meeting: the averted eyes, the quick nods, the heavy quiet. They weren't lazy. They were scared.

"So where do I start?" she asked.

"Start by modelling it," Mel replied. "Tell the truth about what you're seeing, with care. Not as blame, but as clarity. Say, 'Here's what I noticed. Here's why it matters. What are you noticing?' When you do this consistently, you teach your team that candor is safe. And when candor becomes safe, progress speeds up."

Alex wrote the words down: *Candor creates safety. Safety creates capacity.*

For the first time in weeks, she felt like she had a way to cut through the silence. Not with pressure. Not with pretending everything was fine. But with honest, caring clarity.

Chapter 18
Candor

Candor is one of those words that leaders throw around but rarely define. At its core, candor means honest, direct, and respectful communication that creates clarity instead of confusion. It's not about brutal truth-telling or sugar-coating. It's about speaking in a way that makes it easier, not harder, for people to succeed.

In practice, candor often shows up at the crossroads of leadership moments: when something is off-track, when expectations have been misunderstood, or when a tough truth needs to be spoken. Think back to Alex's team in the fable, the missed follow-ups, the mismatched timelines, the awkward silence when asked about progress. That silence wasn't laziness; it was the absence of candor. People didn't know what "good" looked like, and they didn't feel safe enough to say, "I'm unclear." Even though trust was building, candor meant they needed safety beyond that, and they were not sure how far that trust could be tested.

When candor is missing, leaders end up carrying problems in silence until they explode. Teams stay busy but misaligned. Energy goes into politics, workarounds, or rework. But when candor is present, tension gets named early, conflicts are surfaced before they grow, and progress accelerates.

The Difficult Conversations Matrix: Where Conversational Courage and Emotional Intelligence Meet

Every conversation we have lands somewhere on two axes: Conversational Courage (how willing we are to voice the truth) and Emotional Intelligence (how skillfully we express it). Together, these form the Difficult Conversations Matrix.

- **Conversational Courage** is about willingness. Do I step in, or do I stay silent? Do I name the hard thing, or do I let it slide?
- **Emotional Intelligence (EQ)** is about skill. Do I choose words that connect or words that cut? Do I manage my impulses, empathize with others, and express myself in a way that builds trust?

When one axis is strong and the other is weak, conversations can go sideways. (see appendix 9)

Low EQ and High Courage Blunt and Harmful	**High EQ and High Courage** Courageous Connector
Low EQ and Low Courage Silent and Resentful	**High EQ and Low Courage** Empathetic Avoider

Silent & Resentful (Low Courage, Low EQ)

This style is defined by avoidance. Communicators in this quadrant stay quiet in the moment but let resentment and frustration build. Their EQ subscales often show gaps in assertiveness (difficulty voicing needs), emotional expression (withholding feelings), and self-regard (believing their perspective doesn't matter). In meetings, they nod in agreement but later roll their eyes or complain privately. They let mistakes slide without raising concerns, only to vent in side conversations. Over time, they withdraw more and more into silence. When asked for feedback, they respond with vague phrases like, "It's fine, don't worry about it," even when it clearly isn't. Or they remain silent altogether, forcing others to guess their true feelings. At extreme levels, this can turn into gossip and back-channel conversations. Instead of addressing issues directly, they talk about people rather than to them, fueling mistrust and damaging culture.

Empathetic Avoider (High EQ, Low Courage)

This style is defined by care without candor. Communicators here score high on empathy and interpersonal relationships but struggle with assertiveness. They worry that being direct will hurt feelings, so they sugar-coat or avoid hard truths. They comfort a struggling colleague but never clarify what's falling short. They overload themselves with work to avoid confronting others. They create a positive atmosphere on the surface, but progress stalls underneath. People in this quadrant say, "You're doing such a great job, don't stress about the deadline," even though the deadline was critical. Or, "It's not that big of a deal," when it actually is. The greatest risk here is when the leader enables and accepts underperformance. By avoiding accountability, they protect feelings in the short term but create confusion and frustration in the long term.

Blunt & Harmful (High Courage, Low EQ)

This style is defined by honesty without empathy. Communicators in this quadrant often score high on assertiveness but low on impulse control and empathy. They say what's on their mind without considering tone, timing, or impact. They interrupt in meetings to correct others harshly. They send "fix it" emails filled with frustration. They believe in "just being honest" but leave a trail of bruised relationships. Often not realizing the impact of their words, because their intention is not usually bad, they say things like, "This is sloppy," instead of, "This doesn't meet the standard we agreed on. Let's fix it." Or, "You always mess this up," instead of, "Here's what needs to change," with speed often winning out over consideration. At the extremes, this quadrant can look like public shaming, criticism without coaching, and the creation of fear. People stop taking risks or raising concerns because they don't want to be humiliated.

Courageous Connector (High Courage, High EQ)

This style is defined by balancing candor with care. Communicators here leverage multiple EQ subscales: assertiveness (naming the truth), empathy (understanding impact), impulse control (choosing words carefully), and problem solving (focusing on solutions). They address issues promptly and privately. They recognize effort while clarifying gaps. They create space for dialogue, listening as much as they speak. When they communicate, they say things like, "I appreciate the effort you put into this. Here's where it fell short of the standard, and here's what we can do together to close the gap." Or, "I noticed this deadline was missed. What got in the way, and how can I support you to hit it next time?" They model candor as clarity. They show that being direct and being caring are not opposites. Over time, they create cultures where feedback is expected, not feared.

Building Candor Into Leadership Practice

Candor isn't about a single conversation; it's about patterns. To lead with candor, focus on three practices:

Practice Self-Awareness

Candor starts with awareness, of yourself, not just others. You can't practise open, honest communication if you don't understand what gets in your own way. Do you lean toward silence when things get tense? Do you rush conversations to avoid discomfort? Or do you speak so quickly that your message loses empathy along the way?

For many leaders, the real barriers to candor aren't capability; they're patterns, fear of conflict, lack of assertiveness, or the sheer speed of day-to-day demands that leave little room for reflection. As Kim Scott points out in *Radical Candor*, leaders consistently overestimate how open and clear they are, while employees hesitate to share honest feedback out of fear of repercussions.

Awareness is the first act of Candor. When you slow down long enough to notice your default tendencies, you create the space to choose a more intentional response, one that balances honesty with humanity.

Practice: Before your next difficult conversation, write down what you're feeling, the story you're telling yourself about the person, and the assumption you're making. Then ask: *Have I actually said this out loud before?*

Lead With Curiosity

Curiosity disarms defensiveness. Instead of blaming, it opens the door to dialogue. This aligns with the impulse control and reality testing subscales of emotional intelligence: pausing to check assumptions before reacting.

In conscious leadership, this is often described as Above the Line and Below the Line thinking. When we're below the line, we're defensive, closed, or certain, focused on being right rather than learning. When we're above the line, we're curious, open, and willing to see multiple perspectives. The shift may only take a breath, but it transforms the outcome. Leaders who can pause long enough to ask, "Am I above or below the line right now?" create space for emotional regulation and understanding.

Curiosity isn't passive; it's a skill that requires self-management and humility. It asks us to release judgment and lean into learning. Next time something slips, instead of asking, "Why did this happen?" - which can sound accusatory. Try, "What got in the way?" or, "How do you see this situation?" Then repeat back what you heard to confirm understanding. Notice how much more information surfaces when you lead with curiosity instead of certainty.

In Practice: Pause and check in with yourself during your next challenging conversation:

- When tension rises, do you notice yourself closing off or defending your position?
- Can you shift above the line by asking a question instead of making a statement?
- What happens to the energy in the conversation when you replace judgment with genuine curiosity?

The goal isn't to stay "above the line" all the time; it's to notice more quickly when you've fallen below it and consciously choose to rise.

Make Candor a Cultural Norm

Candor doesn't become culture through a single brave conversation; it becomes culture through repetition, modelling, and emotional safety. It's built every time a leader invites truth instead of defending against it. Leaders who normalize candor through vulnerability signal to their teams: "It's safe to be honest here."

This begins with awareness of your own comfort zone. Some leaders talk easily about mistakes but struggle to receive feedback. Others offer feedback freely but resist hearing it. Making candor cultural means practising both, giving and receiving openness with equal courage.

Candor also needs ritual to take root. The most psychologically safe teams don't just talk about honesty; they make space for it. Try ending your next meeting by asking, "What's one thing I could have done better as your leader today?" At first, you may get polite silence. That's normal. Stay consistent. Keep asking. Over time, your team will believe you truly want to know. And that belief, not the question itself, is what creates cultural change.

In Practice: Candor takes practice, not perfection. Pause and ask yourself:

- Which is harder for me: giving honest feedback or receiving it? Why?
- When someone offers me feedback, do I get curious, or do I start preparing my defense?
- How can I show my team that honesty is not a risk, but a value?

The more you explore your own edges with candor, the easier it becomes to model courage for others. Psychological safety doesn't start with policies; it starts with permission. And that permission begins with you.

Reflection & Action

- Where do you sit on the Difficult Conversations Quadrant: Silent & Resentful, Empathetic Avoider, Blunt & Harmful, or Courageous Connector? Where would your team place you?
- What EQ subscales drive your style? For example, does low impulse control push you toward bluntness? Does low assertiveness keep you quiet? Does high empathy without problem solving keep you in avoider mode?
- What's one conversation you've been avoiding? Write down what you'd say in each quadrant style. Then write the Courageous Connector version. Notice how tone changes everything.
- What rituals will you create? Weekly retrospectives, one-on-one check-ins, or end-of-meeting feedback questions can all normalize candor.

Candor is not confrontation. Candor is clarity. And when clarity is paired with care, people not only know where they stand, they know how to win.

Chapter 19
The Ownership Impact

Alex sat at the head of the conference table, laptop open, as her team filed in. She had prepared carefully for this meeting, no vague timelines, no undefined responsibilities. Clarity was her focus, and today she wanted to take it a step further.

"Thanks for coming," Alex began. "Before we jump into updates, I'd like each of us to share one thing that went well this past week and one thing we could improve. Not to blame, but to learn."

The team exchanged uncertain glances. Silence hung in the air for a moment before Priya leaned forward.

"I'll start," she said. "I dropped the ball on one of the client follow-ups. I thought I'd sent the summary, but I got distracted and never hit send. That's on me. To fix it, I've set up an email reminder system so it doesn't happen again."

Alex felt a flicker of relief. *That's ownership*, she thought. Priya hadn't just acknowledged the gap; she had built a solution.

Jamie nodded. "I realized I was behind on my part of the report. I should have asked for help sooner, so I'm adjusting how I block my time. Next week, I'll check in midweek instead of waiting until Friday."

The energy shifted. One by one, people shared not just mistakes but strategies to improve. The mood lightened, and the conversation felt productive instead of painful.

Then it was Marco's turn. He shrugged. "Honestly, I'm just terrible with email. Always have been. Stuff slips through; it's just how I am."

The room went quiet again.

Priya glanced at Alex, waiting. Alex wanted to say something encouraging, but the moment slipped away. They moved on, but the weight lingered.

After the meeting, Alex called Mel.

"Most of the team really stepped up," Alex said. "They weren't just admitting mistakes; they were taking ownership, creating fixes. But Marco... he just threw up his hands. 'That's how I am.' No strategy, no effort to change."

Mel was quiet for a beat. "That's the difference between accountability and ownership. Accountability is saying, 'Yes, I missed the deadline.' Ownership is saying, 'And here's what I'm doing so it doesn't happen again.'"

Alex rubbed her forehead. "So how do I encourage ownership without embarrassing people who resist it?"

"By modelling it, reinforcing it, and connecting it to integrity," Mel replied. "Accountability is responsibility, it's showing up when you're called. Ownership is initiative, stepping up before you're asked. Integrity is when your actions match your words. That's what transforms a culture from doing the minimum to driving real change."

Alex scribbled the words in her notebook: *Accountability = responsibility. Ownership = initiative. Integrity = alignment of words and actions.*

She felt the movement beginning. Now, her job was to help it spread.

Chapter 20
From Accountability to Ownership

Accountability and ownership are often used interchangeably, but they're not the same.

- **Accountability** is responsibility. It's keeping your commitments and answering for results, and it is often driven by another person.
- **Ownership** is initiative. It's integrity in action: aligning words and behaviours, stepping forward without waiting to be asked, and actively creating solutions instead of repeating excuses. It is led by self-motivation rather than social motivation.

Accountability is showing up when called. Ownership is stepping up before anyone has to ask.

Why Ownership Matters

Ownership shifts the culture of a team. When people stop saying, "That's just how I am," and start saying, "Here's how I'm adapting," performance transforms. Take Marco's example. Saying, "I'm bad at email; that's just who I am," is accountability without ownership. He admitted the problem but offered no solution. Compare that to Priya, who said, "I missed a follow-up, so I created a reminder system to prevent it next time." That's ownership: acknowledging the gap and building a fix.

Gallup research shows that employees who feel a sense of ownership are four times more likely to be engaged at work. They don't just comply; they contribute. They innovate, adapt, and go beyond their job description because they feel responsible not just for tasks but for outcomes. Ownership is what turns compliance into commitment.

Ownership and Emotional Intelligence

Ownership is more than a process or a policy. It's a mindset, one grounded in emotional intelligence. Emotional intelligence is what turns self-awareness into accountability, and accountability into action. It's the skill that lets you understand yourself, manage your reactions, and connect meaningfully with others. The EQ-i model breaks this into five composites that show up in every moment of ownership. When they're out of balance, accountability stays surface-level: people admit problems but don't fix them. When they're strong, ownership becomes natural. It's simply how things are done.

Self-Perception: Seeing Yourself Clearly

Ownership begins with a mirror, not a meeting. You can't lead what you can't see.

Leaders with healthy self-regard recognize both their strengths and their blind spots. One of my favourite leaders once said, "I'm allergic to details," and instead of hiding behind it, she built systems to keep herself accountable: a checklist, reminders, and a teammate who thrived on precision. That's self-regard in action, awareness paired with adjustment.

Self-actualization keeps ownership alive. It's the inner voice that says, "I can get better at this." Research from Gallup shows that employees who feel they're learning and growing are nearly 50% less likely to experience high stress and far more engaged at work. Growth and ownership work hand in hand; when one expands, the other strengthens.

And then there's emotional self-awareness: the ability to name what you're feeling before it names you. Without it, frustration turns into defensiveness. With it, you can pause long enough to say, "I was overwhelmed and missed the deadline. Here's how I'll manage things differently next time." That's the foundation of ownership: honest reflection and forward motion.

Self-Expression: Speaking Up and Owning It

Once you understand yourself, ownership means saying it out loud, clearly and constructively.

Assertiveness is the courage to voice your perspective respectfully. It's saying, "I missed a step, but here's how I'll fix it," instead of waiting to be called out. People trust leaders who put commitments into words because it signals accountability without ego.

Independence is the other half. It's taking initiative instead of waiting for someone else to step in. Imagine two employees who both struggle with overflowing inboxes. One sighs, "I'm just terrible at email," and leaves it there. The other says, "I've built filters, blocked time twice a day, and turned off notifications when I need to focus." Both saw the problem, but only one turned awareness into ownership. Ownership requires voice. It's about saying what you'll do, and then doing it.

Interpersonal: Understanding the Ripple Effect

Ownership doesn't happen in isolation. Everything you do, or don't do, affects someone else.

Empathy is recognizing that your choices impact beyond your desk. When you miss a handoff, it's not just your delay; it's someone else's frustration, workload, or missed deadline down the line. Leaders with empathy don't just apologize; they repair. They ask, "What did this impact, and how can I make it right?"

Social responsibility builds on that. Deloitte found that organizations with strong cultures of responsibility see 30% higher retention because people feel their work matters. Ownership thrives in these environments because success is shared. It's no longer "I missed it, my bad," but "I missed it, and here's how I'll adjust so the team succeeds next time."

That shift from "me" to "we" is where accountability transforms into leadership.

Decision-Making: Turning Awareness Into Action

Awareness is powerful, but ownership means doing something with it. Decision-making is where accountability becomes movement. It's where leaders use emotional intelligence not just to think clearly, but to act wisely. Strong decision-makers balance three EQ skills: problem-solving, reality testing, and impulse control.

Problem-solving is about curiosity over control. It's asking, "What's really causing this?" instead of jumping to fix what's on the surface. A leader might notice a client project is constantly behind schedule. The easy answer is to push the team harder or add more meetings. But ownership looks deeper. Maybe the bottleneck isn't effort; it's an unclear approval process or misaligned expectations. Leaders who practise this form of EQ don't just react; they investigate. They trade quick fixes for lasting solutions.

Reality testing keeps you grounded in facts when emotions run high. It's that moment when you pause and say, "What do I actually know to be true?" instead of, "What do I feel is true?" Maybe you're convinced your team is "burnt out," but when you look closer, the issue isn't burnout, it's a lack of clarity or conflicting priorities. EQ-driven leaders don't rely on gut feeling alone. They use data, feedback, and honest dialogue to align perception with reality.

And then there's impulse control, the hardest one for many of us. It's the ability to pause before reacting, to listen without preparing your defense, to replace "That's not true!" with "Tell me more, what are you seeing that I might be missing?"

That small pause changes everything. It's the space where self-awareness turns into growth, and emotion becomes wisdom.

Good decision-making isn't about always being right; it's about staying responsive instead of reactive. Ownership in this space means being brave enough to look beyond the obvious and patient enough to stay in the process until you find the real solution.

Stress Management: Staying the Course When It's Hard

The real measure of ownership isn't how you lead when things are easy; it's how you show up when everything feels heavy.

Stress doesn't reveal new behaviours; it amplifies the ones already there. Under pressure, flexible leaders adapt, while rigid ones double down. Those who practise emotional intelligence don't ignore stress; they manage their energy through it.

Flexibility is the art of adjusting without losing your core. When one strategy stops working, ownership sounds like, "That approach isn't landing, let's try something else." It's not failure; it's agility.

Stress tolerance is emotional endurance. It's the ability to stay steady when the pressure mounts and still make thoughtful choices. I once coached a manager who said, "I can't control the deadline, but I can control how I pace my team." That's ownership under pressure, not denying the stress, but managing it consciously.

And then there's optimism, not blind positivity, but the belief that challenges can be overcome. Martin Seligman's research on optimism shows that people who view setbacks as temporary and specific recover faster and perform better. Optimistic leaders don't dismiss problems; they frame them with possibility. They say, "This is tough, but it's solvable." That mindset keeps teams grounded in hope, even in uncertainty.

Ownership under stress isn't about being unshakable; it's about being real, present, and consistent. It's remembering that your calm becomes their calm. Your tone becomes their tone. Your belief that "we can figure this out" gives everyone permission to keep trying.

In the end, ownership is never about perfection. It's about presence. It's choosing curiosity over control, reflection over reaction, and resilience over rigidity. Leaders with emotional intelligence don't just hold people accountable; they build environments where growth is expected, mistakes are owned, and integrity is visible. And that's what turns good teams into great ones.

Integrity as the Link

Accountability and ownership both live under the banner of integrity. Integrity is when your actions match your words. Accountability says, "I promised to send the report; I'll send it." Ownership says, "I missed the report, but I've changed my workflow so it won't happen again." One is responsibility. The other is growth.

Together, they build trust, because trust is built when words and actions align over time. Trust is broken when people take accountability repeatedly but don't own their commitment to change. Ownership doesn't grow just because a leader demands it; it grows when leaders create an environment where it's safe to take initiative and expected to follow through. If you support the team with strategies to do this, they will be more likely to execute.

Ask Ownership Questions

The questions you ask matter, as they shape the answers you will get. When leaders ask, "Who didn't do this?" the conversation immediately moves into blame. People shrink back; they may point fingers or even go silent. The result is a defensive culture where the real issues stay hidden.

When leaders instead ask, "What part of this can you control? What action can you take right now?" the focus shifts from blame to solution. Suddenly, people are thinking about agency, not guilt. They're moving forward instead of looking backward.

Harvard Business Review has found that employees in solution-focused environments report 31% higher satisfaction and 23% more innovation than those in blame-heavy cultures. By asking solution-focused questions, leaders teach teams to see themselves as active problem-solvers, not passive victims of circumstance.

Create Shared Commitments

Commitments carry more weight when they're spoken out loud. At the end of meetings, I encourage leaders to have each person state what they commit to: "I'll draft the proposal by Wednesday. I'll review the data for accuracy by Friday."

This may sound small, but there's a psychological principle at work here: public commitments increase follow-through. A study in behavioural psychology showed that people who verbalized their goals in front of others were 65% more likely to achieve them. Saying it aloud makes it real. There are principles in the six sources of influence that connect this to what is essentially social peer pressure to perform.

Shared commitments also build collective accountability. Instead of one person quietly holding all the expectations in their head, the whole team knows who owns what. When ownership is visible, it becomes a shared standard, not a hidden burden.

Celebrate Proactive Problem-Solving

Too often, recognition only goes to outcomes, the closed sale, the finished project, the big win. But outcomes are lagging indicators. If you want ownership to become a habit, you need to celebrate the leading behaviours that create outcomes. That means noticing when someone catches a mistake early, proposes a new process, or takes initiative before being asked.

Saying, "I appreciate how you flagged that risk before it escalated," reinforces that ownership isn't just about success; it's about stepping up along the way. Gallup data shows that employees who receive recognition at least once a week are five times more likely to feel engaged. But it's not just frequency that matters, it's specificity. General praise fades fast. Specific recognition, especially for proactive behaviours, teaches people what to repeat.

Use "After-Action" Reviews

Ownership is strengthened through reflection. After a project or milestone, gather the team and ask three questions:

- What went well?
- What didn't?
- What will we do differently next time?

This simple framework, used widely in the military and now adopted by organizations worldwide, keeps conversations forward-looking. Instead of dwelling on failure or assigning blame, "after-action" reviews focus on learning. Research by the U.S. Army found that units using consistent "after-action" reviews improved performance 25% more rapidly than those that didn't.

Ownership was built into the rhythm of reflection. People didn't just admit gaps; they committed to new behaviours for the future. When teams normalize these reviews, accountability conversations lose their sting. Instead of a rare, high-stakes event, feedback becomes a continuous cycle of learning. Ownership is no longer the exception; it's the culture. From an EQ and psychological safety perspective, shifting from blame to learning, and embedding that shift into the culture, is critical.

Ownership questions, shared commitments, proactive recognition, and reflective reviews all work together to build capacity. They shift teams from a culture of compliance, "Did I do what I was told?" to a culture of initiative: "What can I own to help us succeed?"

When leaders use these practices, ownership stops being a slogan on a poster and becomes the way the team delivers.

Reflection & Action

- Where in your life do you stop at accountability but fail to step into ownership?
- What habits have you excused with "That's just how I am"? How could you adapt your strategies instead?
- How often do you align your words and actions? Do others see your integrity in practice?
- This week, choose one area where you've been relying on accountability alone. Take ownership by designing a solution, not just naming the problem.

Because accountability keeps us aligned. Ownership moves us forward. And when a leader builds a culture of ownership, they no longer have to push the team from behind. The team starts pulling the mission forward together.

Chapter 21
The Fog Clears

The office felt different that morning.

Not louder or busier, but lighter, as if someone had finally opened the windows after a long winter.

Alex walked past the team area and noticed something unusual: laughter. Priya and Jamie were reviewing a client report, debating font choices like it was a life-or-death matter. Marco was on a call, but instead of sounding defensive, he was listening, actually listening, and taking notes.

A few months ago, this same team had been weighed down by confusion, silence, and blame. Now, things flowed.

When the weekly team meeting began, Alex didn't need to prompt discussion. Jamie kicked off: "I wanted to flag something early, the new proposal timeline might conflict with the client's internal review cycle. If we move our draft up two days, we'll avoid the crunch."

Alex smiled. "Good catch. What do you guys think?"

Priya jumped in. "I'll take the first draft. Jamie can review. That gives Marco time for client follow-up before Friday."

It was the kind of easy coordination that used to feel impossible.

After the meeting, Alex lingered, watching her team disperse. The old confusion, the hesitations, the unspoken frustrations, had lifted. Everyone was clearer about what mattered, who owned what, and how to course-correct when things slipped.

Mel's words echoed in her mind: *Clarity is kindness. Accountability is alignment. Ownership is integrity in action.*

Later that afternoon, she called Mel.

"I think it's happening," Alex said. "The team's finally in a rhythm. They're problem-solving on their own, catching things before I even notice them."

Mel chuckled. "That's when you know culture has taken root. It's no longer dependent on your presence; it's baked into how they think."

Alex hesitated. "So... what's next? It feels like we've built trust, accountability, ownership, but I can't shake the feeling there's another level. Something beyond the people."

"There is," Mel said. "You've built the human foundation. Now it's time to build the system that sustains it."

"The system?"

"Yes. Leadership systems, the rhythms, the rituals, and the structures, that make sure the culture outlives the moment. That's where most leaders stop short. They think relationships alone will hold it all together. But without systems, culture eventually leaks somewhere."

Alex grabbed her notebook. "Okay," she said, smiling. "Teach me about systems."

Chapter 22
Designing Systems for People

Every high-performing team needs to know two things:

1. Where the boundaries are, and
2. What it takes to win within them.

Processes and systems do both. They define the guardrails that keep people safe and the pathways that help them succeed. Systems aren't about control; they are about clarity. They let your team know how far they can stretch, how decisions get made, and what success looks like in practice. Without clear systems, people guess. They hesitate, overcommunicate, or wait for permission. With them, people act with confidence, creativity, and purpose. And as we'll explore in future chapters, these same systems, when designed with emotional intelligence, don't just improve productivity. They make sure everyone knows how to win together.

The Shift from People-Dependent to System-Supported

When a team relies only on relationships, everything flows through individual effort. It feels human, until someone gets tired. When things get busy or stressful, consistency drops, communication breaks down, and culture starts to wobble. System-supported cultures are different. They still prioritize people, but they back them up with structure and routines that protect trust and energy. It's not about bureaucracy; it's about building intentionality into how work gets done.

I am a firm believer that "Strong leaders build culture through connection. Great leaders sustain it through structure." I want you to consider systems and structures differently. What if they were designed to support energy systems? What if they were meant for people to thrive versus the organization to control? How would they be different? Let's explore this concept further.

Physical Energy: Design for Capacity, Not Exhaustion

Physical energy is about how we spend our time and attention. Workload, scheduling, and capacity all live here. A system that ignores physical energy burns people out. A system that honours it plans around how humans actually function.

An example of this is a large insurance firm that introduced "90-minute focus zones" twice a week, where meetings and emails were paused. Productivity rose by 28%, and burnout reports fell by nearly half within three months (Gartner, 2023).

You can do this by building recovery into the workflow: shorter meetings, realistic project pacing, and protected time for deep work. Deloitte found that employees who manage their energy, not just their hours, are 45% more engaged and 56% more likely to stay for over two years.

When you consider physical energy, you ask: Are we working people to their limits, or designing work so they can sustain excellence?

Mental Energy: Design for Clarity, Focus, and Autonomy

Mental energy fuels focus and creativity. It's what allows people to make good decisions, solve problems, and stay mentally present at work. But most workplaces unintentionally drain it. Every "ping," "ding," and "quick question" fractures attention, and the average employee now switches tasks every three minutes, taking over 20 minutes to refocus (UC Irvine, 2023).

Ironically, tools meant to boost productivity often lower it by flooding people with notifications and interruptions. A people-centred system designs for attention, not distraction.

An example of this was a marketing firm adopting "batching" practices. Instead of constant messages, they saved non-urgent items for 30-minute collaboration blocks. Productivity improved by 31%, and stress dropped by nearly half. As leaders, we need to recognize when we are contributing to the problem.

Before interrupting someone, ask, "Does this need to be right now, or can it wait for our next check-in?" This single habit protects cognitive energy across the team. Microsoft found that employees with uninterrupted focus time are 121% more likely to say they're performing at their best. Who wouldn't want this type of result?

Give people freedom within frameworks. Let them design how they work, as long as clarity on outcomes remains constant. When we consider mental energy in systems, we ask: Are we designing for flow, or for constant friction?

Emotional Energy: Design for Trust and Belonging

Emotional energy is about how people feel at work, about their leader, their team, and the organization itself. Systems have emotional impact. A confusing performance review process erodes trust. A transparent feedback loop builds it.

So much of what we have talked about up to this point aligns here. Our role as leaders is to build trust that sets our teams up for success. A marketing agency replaced annual reviews with quarterly "growth conversations." Each session began with, "What do you need to do your best work?" Satisfaction rose by 40%, and turnover dropped by 25%.

What would happen if you audited policies for emotional impact? Ask yourself, "Does this process make people feel trusted and valued, or anxious and watched?" The Edelman Trust Barometer (2024) found that 79% of employees are more engaged when they trust leadership and feel psychological safety. You need to ask yourself: Do our structures protect trust, or quietly damage it?

Spiritual Energy: Design for Meaning and Alignment

Spiritual energy connects people to purpose, ensuring they know why the work matters. Systems that ignore this leave people feeling like they are just cogs in a machine. Systems that connect to purpose turn ordinary tasks into meaningful contributions.

This can be a simple focus shift. For example, a healthcare organization redesigned onboarding to begin with patient impact stories instead of compliance paperwork. New hires reported a 72% higher sense of purpose within 30 days (McKinsey, 2023).

When you tie every system back to "why," or connect each task to its purpose, who it helps, why it matters, and how it contributes to something larger, systems don't feel as much like systems; they feel more like intentions. McKinsey found that employees who find purpose at work are five times more likely to be engaged and twice as likely to stay long-term.

So, as you evaluate your systems, ask: Does our process remind people why their work matters, or just tell them what to do?

Reflection & Action: Auditing Your Systems for Human Energy

Before you can improve your systems, you have to see them clearly. Use these prompts to start your own audit:

1. **Boundaries & Clarity:** Do your systems make it clear where people have freedom to act versus where they need alignment? Reflect on the learnings up until now that can help in this instance.

2. **Physical Energy:** Do your workflows create a sustainable pace, or reward exhaustion?

3. **Mental Energy:** Are tools and communication channels supporting focus, or stealing it?
4. **Emotional Energy:** Does feedback build trust or tension?
5. **Spiritual Energy:** Can every system answer, "Why does this matter?"

To go deeper, use the detailed People-First Systems Audit in the worksheet to evaluate how your organization aligns with the four energy systems. (see appendix 10)

Part Three
Everybody Wins

Turning Clarity into Collective Success

When people know how to win, they stay. When they stay, the business thrives.

This part is about alignment, connecting people, purpose, and performance. Alex learns how to tie expectations to shared values, how to create clarity across teams and departments, and how to build systems that support growth without losing humanity.

You'll see how emotional intelligence shapes customer experience, sales, and organizational success. Because when leaders align clarity with care, everybody wins, the people, the customers, and the company.

Chapter 23
The Customer Connection

The morning sunlight streamed through the office windows as Alex reviewed the latest customer satisfaction scores. They weren't bad, but they weren't great either. There was one comment that caught her eye:

"The team was kind, but I didn't always know what to expect next."

It wasn't criticism exactly. But it landed heavy.

A few months ago, Alex would have brushed it off, another number on a dashboard. But now, she paused. Kind, but unclear. It sounded a lot like her team before they'd started aligning their own expectations.

That afternoon, she met with her team. "We've done a lot of work on building trust, accountability, and ownership," she began. "Now, I think it's time to extend that same clarity to our customers."

Priya nodded. "I feel like sometimes we overdeliver in one area but forget to close the loop somewhere else."

"Exactly," Alex said. "Customers should never have to guess what's happening next. They deserve the same consistency and transparency we expect from each other."

Marco raised his hand. "So, are we talking about new scripts or templates?"

Alex smiled. "Not exactly. I think we're talking about how we show up, our mindset. Let's think about the customer journey the same way we've thought about our team journey."

She drew a pie chart on the whiteboard.

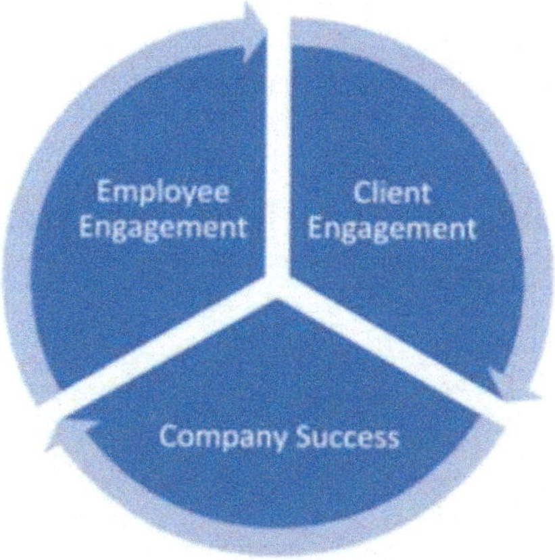

"When we take care of each other, like we have been doing," she said, "we show up energized and confident. We need that energy to flow to the customer. When customers feel cared for, they will come back, and the organization thrives."

Jamie leaned forward. "So... it's not just customer service. It's the experience the customer feels, built from the inside out."

"Exactly," Alex said. "It's the Everybody Wins Method in action. Our goal is to create an experience that adds a 'deposit' to a jar of trust. We need to make sure we are always adding to that jar; this way, when we make a mistake, because we are human, the trust jar is still full."

Over the next few weeks, the team put this into practice. They started small: clear follow-up notes after every meeting, proactive updates when timelines shifted, and one simple but powerful new phrase:

"Here's what you can expect next."

It became their new trust deposit.

Within a month, feedback shifted. Customers used words like *consistent, easy, confident, cared for.*

One even wrote:

"I felt like they were two steps ahead of me, in a good way."

Alex smiled when she read it. That was it. That was what leadership done right looked like, not just inside the walls of her team, but everywhere their work reached.

Everybody really could win.

Chapter 24
The Everybody Wins Method

Most companies measure success in numbers: revenue, retention, and customer satisfaction, etc. But behind every number is an ecosystem of people. The Everybody Wins Method is about building that ecosystem intentionally, where your people, your customers, and your organization thrive together. It starts inside and expands outward:

(see appendix 11)

Take Care of Your Team

When people feel valued, trusted, and empowered, they perform better and care more. Gallup's 2024 *State of the Workplace* report found that highly engaged employees lead to 23% higher profitability and 81% lower absenteeism. But engagement doesn't come from perks or slogans. It comes from leadership that meets people's emotional and operational needs, the very foundation of *The Happy Leader Method*. It's what we have been building toward throughout this book. It's Energize, Prioritize, Optimize, and Build Great Relationships, applied daily. It's giving people clear expectations, consistent feedback, and meaningful purpose. When you take care of your team, they don't just do their jobs. They own them.

Take Care of Your Customers

Every customer interaction is an emotional experience. Whether they're buying a coffee, signing a contract, or renewing a service, they're deciding if the value they received matches or exceeds the effort and cost they invested. Value isn't just about price; it's about how people feel when they buy from you.

Take coffee, for example. The cost of beans in a cup of specialty coffee might be less than 50 cents. Yet customers regularly spend \$5–\$8 because they aren't paying for caffeine, they're paying for the experience. The music, the smell, the personalization, the barista remembering their name, that's value. It transforms a commodity into a connection.

In business, every organization must decide what they want their experience to be. There is no wrong answer. It's about deciding and then delivering that experience consistently.

Are we high value, low cost: fast, accessible, and efficient?

Are we moderate cost, consistent experience: dependable, reliable, and easy to work with?

Or are we a premium experience: high investment, high touch, and deeply personalized?

Like I said, there is no wrong answer, but there *is* wrong alignment. When asking yourself these questions, you are comparing yourself to others in your own market. If your brand promises a "premium partnership" but your internal systems are built for speed and volume, customers will feel the disconnect. Likewise, if your team is structured for bespoke care but your pricing and staffing are built for efficiency, frustration builds on both sides.

Clarity about your value promise, what you want your customer to experience, is clarity for your team. It shapes hiring, processes, communication, and service design. In short, your internal systems must reflect your external promise. You can't deliver a five-star experience with two-star alignment. When your team understands exactly what you want your customers to feel, they can design actions that make that emotion predictable, every time.

The Customer Journey and the Feeling Framework

The best customer experiences aren't accidental; they're engineered for emotion. Great leaders know that what customers remember most isn't what you said or did, it's how you made them feel. And that feeling is built long before they ever buy from you. When you intentionally design your customer journey around emotion, you create experiences that feel effortless, personal, and human, the kind people come back for and tell others about.

Discovery / First Contact → From Curious to Confident

(see appendix 12)

This is the moment your customer first meets you, online, in person, through a referral, or on social media. It's where curiosity turns into a decision: *Do I trust this person, this product, this company?* At this stage, your goal is simple: replace uncertainty with clarity.

When your communication is clear, kind, and consistent, people start to relax. They shift from "Can I trust them?" to "I think I can." This looks like a potential client visiting your website and easily understanding what you do, who you help, and how to take the next step. Or a first conversation that starts with warmth instead of pressure.

This sounds like: "Here's how we can help, and what you can expect if we work together." Even in digital spaces, tone matters. If your email response times are unpredictable or your marketing messages overpromise, curiosity fades into confusion.

Confidence grows when every touchpoint says, "We know what we're doing, and we've got you."

Engagement / Decision → From Supported to Secure

Once curiosity becomes interest, the next emotion your customer needs is security. This is where they're comparing, questioning, or deciding whether to move forward. Many organizations lose trust here because they focus on selling rather than supporting.

The emotionally intelligent approach is different: you guide, you listen, you clarify, you don't convince. This looks like a sales conversation focused on understanding the customer's goals, not defending your offer. This sounds like: "Here's what I recommend based on what you've told me, and if it's not the right fit, I'll tell you that too."

This level of candor creates psychological safety for customers. They feel secure knowing you care about the right solution, not just the sale. And here's where leadership mirrors customer experience: just as employees need clear expectations to feel safe, customers need clarity to feel confident signing on. When your communication is transparent, pricing, process, timelines, the decision becomes a natural next step, not a leap of faith.

Delivery / Service → From Valued to Delighted

The delivery stage is where trust is tested. Promises made become promises kept, or broken. Here, emotional intelligence shows up in follow-through. Customers should feel both valued and seen.

The team's consistency, communication, and care determine whether this stage feels like a partnership or a transaction. This looks like a team proactively updating a client before they have to ask. Delivering work on time and explaining delays before they become problems. This sounds like: "We're on track for Friday's delivery. Here's what we've completed, and here's what's next."

This is also the moment to infuse humanity into your systems. Automation and tools are useful, but empathy makes them meaningful. Customers should never wonder, "Do they even remember me?"

When leaders design systems that close communication loops, recognize contributions, and personalize touchpoints, customers shift from valued to delighted. And delight isn't about grand gestures; it's about dependability with a touch of care. A personalized thank-you, a quick follow-up, or a small detail remembered. Delight is the emotional outcome of consistent reliability.

Follow-Up / Relationship → From Remembered to Loyal

The sale or service may close, but the relationship is just getting started. This stage is about longevity, turning satisfaction into loyalty. It's where you demonstrate that care isn't conditional on the transaction.

Loyalty is built when customers feel remembered. They see that they matter beyond their invoice. This looks like a follow-up email a week later just to check in. A team remembering a client's milestone and reaching out with congratulations. This sounds like: "We were thinking about you, how's the project working out?" or "I saw something that reminded me of our conversation."

The human brain is wired to remember emotion. That means your customer's last emotional experience defines how they remember your entire relationship. Ending the journey with authenticity, gratitude, and connection transforms customers into advocates, people who not only come back but bring others with them.

When you lead your customer experience with empathy, transparency, and consistency, you don't have to ask for loyalty. You earn it.

Take Care of the Organization

When teams and customers thrive, the organization can focus on sustainable growth.

McKinsey's 2023 research found that companies with top-quartile employee experience outperform peers by 147% in earnings per share. The reason is simple: alignment scales.

A company whose internal culture matches its customer promise doesn't waste energy reconciling the gap between what's said and what's done. Employees aren't pretending to care, they actually do, because their work environment models the same values they deliver outward.

Alex's team had learned that clarity builds trust internally. Now they were living it externally. The consistency in their process became their brand identity. Inside and outside, same values, same experience.

That's what "Everybody Wins" looks like in action.

Why It Works

When you invest in the human side of performance, you create measurable results that last. Customers notice turnover; they are building relationships with you *and* your people, and that matters.

Companies with highly engaged employees experience 20% higher sales and 10% higher customer ratings (Gallup, 2024). Emotionally connected customers have 306% higher lifetime value and are 71% more likely to recommend your brand (Harvard Business Review, 2023). Teams with strong internal communication improve customer satisfaction by up to 50%.

But beyond the numbers, what makes it work is this: customers don't experience your mission statement. They experience your people

When your people are energized, aligned, and emotionally intelligent, every interaction becomes a trust deposit into that jar we talked about, and trust is the only currency that never loses value.

Reflection & Action: Designing Your Customer Experience

1. **Define Your Value Promise:** What do you want your customer to feel? Is your team structure designed to deliver that feeling consistently?

2. **Map the Emotional Journey:** Identify each customer stage and the emotion you want to evoke. Then align systems, language, and follow-up to that goal.
3. **Audit for Alignment:** Review marketing, pricing, and team culture. Are they telling the same story? If your "brand experience" and "employee experience" don't match, customers will feel it first.
4. **Build Feedback Loops:** Celebrate positive customer comments in team meetings. Treat feedback as coaching, not criticism.

When your internal values and external promises align, you don't just create loyal customers, you create advocates. Everybody Wins!

Chapter 25
The Value Misalignment

The office was quiet except for the steady tapping of keyboards.

Alex looked up from her laptop as Priya walked in, balancing two coffees. "Thought you could use this," she said, setting one down.

"Thank you," Alex smiled. "You read my mind."

They'd been in the middle of a major client rollout, one that depended on precision and consistency. Deadlines were tight. Expectations were clear.

Priya's work, as always, was beautiful. Detailed. Thoughtful. Too thoughtful, maybe.

"Hey," Alex said carefully. "Can we chat for a sec about the new proposal?"

Priya nodded, taking a seat. "Of course. I was just about to finalize it, but I wanted to polish a few sections first."

Alex hesitated. "It looks amazing. Really. But the client expected it yesterday. They've been waiting for an update."

Priya frowned. "I know. I just didn't want to send something that wasn't perfect yet."

There it was. That word again.

Perfect.

Alex took a slow breath. "I appreciate your attention to detail, Priya. I really do. But I think we might be measuring success differently."

Priya looked confused. "What do you mean?"

"You hold yourself, and your work, to a level of quality that's exceptional," Alex said. "But the company's promise to clients is consistency and dependability. We've positioned ourselves as a partner who always delivers on time, even if that means 95% perfect instead of 100%."

Priya shifted in her chair. "So, you'd rather it be on time than flawless?"

Alex nodded gently. "I'd rather it be predictable. We win when clients know exactly what to expect from us, no surprises, no delays."

Priya stared at her hands. "That's hard for me. I want our work to stand out."

"And it does," Alex said softly. "But I think we define 'standing out' differently. For you, it's about excellence and perfection. For us, it's excellence and consistency. Both matter; they just lead to different kinds of success."

The silence between them was heavy but honest.

After a moment, Priya asked, "So what does that mean for me?"

"It means I want to understand what motivates you," Alex said. "You're incredibly talented, and I don't want you to feel like you have to lower your standards. But I also don't want you burning yourself out trying to make every project perfect in a company built on consistency, when 'good enough' is sometimes just that: good enough."

Later that week, Alex met with Mel over coffee.

"I think Priya's struggling," Alex said. "Not because she's not capable, she's incredible, but because our values are pulling her in a direction that doesn't feel right to her."

Mel nodded. "So what you're seeing isn't resistance. It's misalignment."

Alex exhaled. "Exactly. She's trying to play a premium game in a consistency-based company. It's not wrong, just different."

Mel leaned in. "Then the question isn't whether she's right for the team. It's whether this team is right for her. Remember, excellence isn't universal. It depends on the rules of the game."

Alex smiled sadly. "You're saying she might need to find a different game."

Mel nodded. "Maybe. But first, make sure you've both defined the rules clearly. Misalignment is often just a lack of shared language."

Alex tilted her head. "Shared language?"

Mel smiled. "Think about it this way: if I say 'excellent service,' what does that mean to you?"

Alex thought for a moment. "I'd say delivering what we promised, on time, with no surprises."

"And for someone else," Mel continued, "it might mean taking extra time to personalize the client experience, going above and beyond every single time. Both of those are valid interpretations of excellence, but if you don't define which one your company stands for, you'll have people rowing in opposite directions, all believing they're doing the right thing."

Alex nodded slowly, the realization landing.

"Shared language," Mel said again. "You can't hold someone accountable to a standard they never agreed to. Until you define what 'good,' 'on time,' or even 'done' means in your world, you're leaving room for everyone to fill in the blanks with their own meanings."

"That's exactly what's happening with Priya," Alex admitted. "She's not wrong; she's just speaking a different dialect of excellence."

Mel grinned. "Exactly. And your job as a leader isn't to tell her she is wrong for that, it's to redefine her belief. Sometimes the gap between misalignment and momentum is just a better conversation."

Alex laughed softly. "So maybe before I decide whether she's playing the wrong position, I should make sure we're even playing the same game."

"Now you've got it," Mel said. "You can't coach someone toward alignment if you're both standing in different definitions of success."

As Alex left the café, she felt the familiar mix of clarity and weight that came with real leadership.

Leadership wasn't just about coaching people to perform. Sometimes, it was about helping them recognize when their best work might belong somewhere else.

Chapter 26
Alignment, Not Perfection

When performance issues surface, we often assume someone isn't trying hard enough. But more often, it's not about effort at all. It's about alignment. Alignment happens when what we value as individuals matches what the organization values as a collective. When it doesn't, even the most talented people can feel stuck or frustrated.

Values in Action, Not Just Words on the Wall

Every organization has values posted somewhere: in a staff handbook, painted on a wall, or written in the annual report. Words like trust, respect, innovation, or excellence appear everywhere. But the truth is, values don't live on the wall. They live in how people behave. The problem isn't that organizations don't have values; it's that they don't define them in action.

One organization I worked with had "trust" as one of its core values. But when we unpacked what trust actually meant there, it wasn't about blind faith or deep emotional connection; it was about consistency. Trust meant creating the same experience every single time: clean spaces, friendly service, and systems that worked. That clarity changed everything. It gave people a playbook. They knew what trust looked like in behaviour, and what it didn't.

The misalignment came when people spent too much time socializing with clients, believing that building personal rapport was trust. They weren't wrong; they were just not aligned. They had different definitions. But the result was uneven experiences for other clients, and in a consistency-driven culture, that eroded trust instead of building it.

Values have to be defined objectively, not philosophically. If you can't describe a value with observable behaviours, you haven't defined it yet. When values are clear and visible, reinforced in onboarding, team meetings, goal setting, recognition programs, and performance conversations, they stop being buzzwords and start being a way of life.

Shared Language: Values as Expectations

Mel was right when she told Alex, "Misalignment is often just a lack of shared language."

Values are, at their core, expectations. They describe how we show up for one another, what we reward, and what we don't. If one person defines quality as "flawless craftsmanship" and another defines it as "delivered on time," both are right, but without alignment, both will feel wrong. Shared language takes those abstract words and turns them into practical expectations. It means we stop assuming people "just know" what we mean.

Instead, we translate:

"For us, trust looks like following through on commitments."

"Respect means giving feedback directly, not gossiping about someone afterward."

"Excellence means consistency, not perfection."

When everyone understands not only what is valued but how it shows up in behaviour, accountability stops being emotional. It becomes clarity in motion.

A simple way to do this is to:

1. Name the value
2. Describe what it means in words
3. Describe what it looks like in action

4. Describe what it does *not* look like in action

The Values–Performance Matrix

Every team has a mix of skill and alignment. (see appendix 13)

High Skill and High Alignment Result: Thrives Leader Focus: Empower and Grow *Shares Values and Performs*	**High Skill and Low Alignment** Result: Friction or flight risk Leader Focus: Clarify values, Coach for alignment *Excellent work but plays by different rules*
Low Skill and High Alignment Result: Growth Opportunity Leader Focus: Train and Develop *Aligned but under skilled*	**Low Skill and Low Alignment** Result: Low trust and low engagement Leader Focus: Compassionate exit *Misfit for role and culture*

Priya's story fits the second box: high skill, low alignment. Her craftsmanship was remarkable, but her version of "great" didn't match the company's definition of success.

And that doesn't make her wrong; it makes her different. The leader's job isn't to fix that difference; it's to clarify it.

Defining Success Together

In emotionally intelligent organizations, alignment replaces perfectionism.

People stop chasing "doing everything right" and start focusing on "doing the right things for us." This mindset allows space for growth. What's "good enough" today may not be what's good enough tomorrow, and that's okay. Alignment evolves as the business evolves.

A start-up might value speed and experimentation; five years later, it might prioritize process and stability. That shift doesn't make early employees wrong; it means the company's definition of success has matured. When leaders communicate this fluidity, when they make it clear that alignment is dynamic, people are more willing to adapt.

They stop fearing change and start participating in it.

The Alignment Conversation: Curiosity Before Correction

The most effective alignment conversations begin with curiosity, not correction. When something feels off, pause before judging performance. Ask questions that uncover why:

- "What does great work mean to you?"
- "What's most important to you about how we do our work here?"
- "Where do you feel most energized, and where do you feel out of sync?"
- "What makes you proud at the end of the day?"

These questions reveal motivations and values beneath the surface. True alignment conversations also require transparency. If you notice a gap, name it kindly:

"I've noticed that your approach values depth and personalization, while our clients value speed and consistency. I want to understand what that feels like for you."

This shifts the conversation from confrontation to collaboration. It allows both leader and employee to decide together whether alignment can be rebuilt, or if a different fit might serve them both better. Candor builds clarity, and clarity creates freedom. Tools from the other chapters can add additional value as you reflect here.

Alignment as Emotional Intelligence in Motion

Emotional intelligence is what allows alignment conversations to work. It's what helps leaders listen without defensiveness and employees respond without fear.

Think of Priya and Alex:

Alex used self-awareness to recognize her own frustration, empathy to understand Priya's perspective, and reality testing to see the organizational truth, that both definitions of excellence were valid but misaligned. Her emotional expression allowed her to communicate that truth clearly but compassionately, and her interpersonal skills built the trust required for an honest dialogue. That's emotional intelligence in action, not theory.

Ownership in Alignment: Work as a Partnership

Alignment isn't a one-way street.

It isn't just the leader's job to define expectations or the company's role to set the tone.

True alignment happens when both sides take ownership, when employees also step forward to understand, question, and shape how their values fit within the organization.

If you ever find yourself feeling disengaged or frustrated at work, it's worth asking the same questions your leader should be asking you:

- "What matters most to me about how we do our work here?"
- "Do I believe in the way success is defined in this organization?"
- "Where am I feeling energized, and where am I feeling out of sync?"
- "Have I shared my perspective clearly, or am I waiting for someone else to notice?"

Ownership means recognizing that "fit" goes both ways. It's not just about whether you meet expectations; it's about whether the environment allows you to thrive as your best self. Psychologist William Kahn's foundational research on engagement found that when employees see their work as a mutual exchange of value, their commitment and satisfaction rise dramatically. When people feel they can influence their environment, they're almost three times more likely to stay engaged and resilient through change.

Taking ownership doesn't mean forcing yourself to adapt at all costs. It means taking responsibility for understanding the system you're in and deciding, with honesty, whether it still aligns with who you're becoming. Work should feel like a partnership.

Both the organization and the individual share responsibility for maintaining alignment, continually checking in, communicating openly, and making adjustments when values or goals evolve. When that partnership is healthy, accountability feels empowering, not oppressive. People stop saying, "They don't get me," and start asking, "How can we better understand each other?"

The Leadership Effect

Even when alignment exists, it's fragile. The arrival of a new leader can change everything. Have you ever noticed how often new leadership leads to waves of resignations or restructures? That's not coincidence; it's misalignment in motion.

Every leader brings their own interpretation of the company's values. A culture built on autonomy can suddenly feel micromanaged. A team that thrived on stability can suddenly be asked to "move fast and break things." This isn't about right or wrong leadership; it's about clarity. When a leader's style and the team's established values diverge, confusion and fatigue follow. That's why every leadership transition should include a values realignment conversation. Ask:

- "What parts of our culture feel essential to keep?"
- "What might we need to evolve under new leadership?"
- "What does success look like now, and how will we measure it?"

Alignment isn't a one-time event; it's an ongoing dialogue. And the organizations that treat it that way retain both their people and their momentum.

Reflection & Action: Leading for Alignment

1. **Audit Your Culture:** What behaviours are rewarded most often? Are they the ones that reflect your stated values?
2. **Define How You Win:** Write down, in one sentence, how your organization defines "great work." Then ask your team to do the same. Compare the answers.
3. **Host Alignment Conversations:** When friction appears, replace correction with curiosity. Ask, "What definition might we be missing here?"

4. **Recognize Value Misfits Early:** A compassionate conversation today prevents disengagement tomorrow. Alignment sometimes means guiding someone to a better fit, inside or outside the team.

5. **Model Integrity:** Let your actions match your words. When your behaviour consistently mirrors your stated values, your team learns alignment by example.

Alignment isn't about sameness; it's about shared direction. Because when people understand how to win in your organization, they don't just work harder, they work together.

Chapter 27
The Courage to Let Go

Alex sat alone in the quiet hum of her office lights. It was after six, that in-between hour when the sunlight faded and the cleaning crew hadn't yet arrived. From her office window, she could see the faint glow of Priya's desk lamp still on. She sighed. Again.

It wasn't the first time Priya had stayed late; in fact, it was becoming routine. Her projects were still hitting deadlines, but only because she was working long after everyone else had gone home. And the rest of the team was starting to notice.

Comments had started surfacing in subtle ways:

"She's amazing, but I don't know how she keeps that pace."

"Do we need to be working that late too?"

"Does this mean my work isn't good enough?"

It wasn't resentment; it was confusion.

Alex had already tried to address it with Priya. She'd encouraged her to prioritize differently, to embrace "done" over "perfect," to find a rhythm that didn't require so much sacrifice. But Priya's standards were rooted in pride, not defiance. Her work was her art.

And Alex respected that, maybe too much.

She glanced at her phone. A message from Mel blinked on the screen:

Don't forget: care isn't always holding on. Sometimes it's letting go.

The next morning, Alex found Priya in the break room, pouring coffee.

"Hey," Alex said softly. "Got a few minutes to talk?"

Priya smiled faintly. "Sure."

They sat in the meeting room together, a quiet stillness between them.

"Priya," Alex began, "I've noticed how much you've been putting into your work. The hours, the detail, it's extraordinary. But I'm worried about the toll it's taking on you."

Priya gave a small laugh, though it didn't reach her eyes. "I'm fine, really. I just want to make sure everything I deliver represents the best of us."

Alex leaned forward. "And it does. But here's what's happening: you're producing excellence at a pace that isn't sustainable, for you or for the team. Your work is exceptional, but it's not aligned with the expectations or capacity of the organization, and that's creating strain. I know you're trying to meet your own expectations, and even though we've talked about those expectations being higher than what the organization requires, it's now starting to be noticed by others and has them questioning their own work."

Priya's shoulders slumped slightly. "I've felt that. I just didn't want to disappoint anyone."

"You haven't," Alex said. "You've done more than anyone could ask. But I think this might be one of those moments where what you need from your work and what we can provide aren't the same anymore."

Priya looked down at her hands. "You mean... maybe it's time?"

Alex nodded slowly. "I think so. Not because you've failed, but because you deserve a place that matches the kind of excellence you want to create, somewhere that measures success the same way you do."

Tears welled in Priya's eyes, but she smiled. "I think you're right. I've been trying to make it fit, but it hasn't felt right for a while."

They spent the next hour talking, not about tasks or deadlines, but about next steps. Alex offered to introduce her to someone she knew at a boutique firm known for high-touch, personalized work. They discussed an exit strategy together that allowed Priya to be supported through the transition.

When Priya left, she paused at the door, took off her access badge, and set it gently on the desk. "Thank you," she said, her voice steady. "For seeing me."

After she left, Alex sat quietly for a long time. It was hard, harder than she'd expected. But it wasn't heavy.

It was honest.

That night, she texted Mel:

It's done. It hurts, but it feels right.

Mel replied: *That's leadership, Alex. You didn't lose anyone; you helped someone win.*

Alex gathered her team the next morning. She didn't fill the silence with corporate phrases or empty reassurances. She simply said:

"Priya and I talked about what's best for her and for us. She's moving on to something that aligns better with her goals. We're grateful for everything she's done here."

This conversation mattered more than any exit interview ever could.

Chapter 28
Exits, Endings, and Ecosystems

Leaders often fear endings. They equate them with failure or loss. But endings, when handled with clarity, care, and integrity, are one of the greatest reflections of culture. When we reach this point, it should never be a surprise. A healthy exit conversation is not an isolated event; it's the culmination of everything that came before it. You've already:

- Set expectations clearly.
- Built relationships grounded in trust and care.
- Had courageous conversations about performance and values.

By the time an exit discussion happens, it's simply the next chapter in a long, honest dialogue. When relationships and transparency are prioritized, people usually see it coming, not because they're being pushed out, but because they've been supported every step of the way. When leaders lead with care, it's not uncommon for an employee to walk into that final meeting already knowing it's time, "handing in their keys," so to speak, before you've asked, because they know you want them to win. And in some cases, they'll already have found their next opportunity, because the clarity you've built helped them realize what's next for them before you even had to say it. That's what leadership looks like when Clarity, Care, and Continuity aren't just tools for exits, but threads that run through every conversation along the way.

The 3 C's of Compassionate Exits, In Every Step of Leadership

Clarity

Clarity doesn't begin in the final conversation. It may start months earlier, through every feedback moment and expectation-setting discussion that came before. Each one is a deposit in the trust bank, small acts of honesty that add up to safety. When the final moment arrives, it isn't an ambush; it's a mutual understanding. In Priya's case, clarity meant reinforcing what success looked like early and often. When Alex finally said, "I think it's time," Priya wasn't blindsided. She felt seen. Clarity in the exit itself means being direct, specific, and kind: "You bring extraordinary value, but what you need from your work no longer matches what we can offer. And that's okay." Leaders who communicate this way turn endings into understanding instead of blame.

Care

Care isn't about sympathy; it's about dignity. Leaders can show care by acknowledging emotions without rushing to fix them: "I know this is hard, and I want you to know I value everything you've contributed here." Alex showed care by staying present, by helping Priya think about what came next, and by ensuring she didn't feel discarded but supported. Care also means remembering that the person leaving has an impact on those who stay. Teams watch how leaders treat people in moments of transition. Every gesture, every tone, every silence sends a message about what kind of organization they work in. When people feel that care is real, they don't just trust you when they're winning; they trust you when things are hard.

Continuity

Continuity is how leaders maintain stability while honouring change. It's the bridge between what was and what's next. That means explaining departures with integrity.

Not gossip. Not avoidance.

When you communicate clearly, without violating privacy, you maintain trust: "We made a mutual decision based on alignment and fit.

We're proud of the work we've done together." Continuity also includes making sure work transitions smoothly, clients are informed respectfully, and remaining team members know where they stand.

Trust Before, During, and After

Exits are emotional for everyone, even when they're handled beautifully.

But what determines whether they weaken or strengthen culture is how leaders manage the trust bank before, during, and after.

Before: Build Consistency and Psychological Safety

Trust begins long before a tough conversation. It's built in how consistently you show up, how transparently you communicate, and how clearly people know what to expect from you. People shouldn't have to guess how you'll react when things get tough. They should already know your style, how you deliver feedback, how you celebrate, and how you coach.

I often tell leaders to be clear about this from the very beginning, even during onboarding. I once worked with a leader who knew self-awareness was her growth edge. She admitted she wasn't naturally great at giving praise and was quick to point out gaps. Instead of pretending otherwise, she owned it from the start. She would say:

"I'm not always great at saying 'great job,' but I promise I'm direct, you'll never be surprised if something isn't working. That said, if recognition motivates you, please tell me. I'll make sure you get it. Thank you for the grace while I work on this."

That kind of vulnerability builds trust instantly. It gave her team permission to ask for what they needed and removed the fear of misreading her tone. Clarity about how you lead is one of the strongest trust deposits you can make.

During: Model Empathy and Regulate Emotion

The moment of an exit conversation tests every ounce of a leader's emotional intelligence. It's not just about what you say; it's about how you say it. Model empathy through your tone, your pace, and your presence. Keep your body language open. Maintain eye contact, but not intensity. Silence your phone, close your laptop, and give the person your full attention. The goal isn't to minimize emotion; it's to create enough safety for it to exist.

One of the most compassionate things you can say in that moment is simply: "I know this is hard, and it's okay to feel that." If emotions rise, resist the instinct to fill space with justification or apology. Listen fully. Breathe. Ground the conversation in mutual respect. Remember: this is not just a transaction; it is a human transition. The way you hold space determines whether that person leaves with dignity or damage. And your team will feel it too. They'll remember not the words, but the energy in the room, whether it felt like blame or grace.

After: Follow Through and Rebuild Stability

Once the door closes, the work isn't over. How you show up after someone leaves is just as important as how you showed up before or during. Follow through on every commitment made in the conversation. If you offered to provide a reference, do it quickly. If you promised an introduction, send it that day. Then, turn your attention to the team that remains.

Transitions change group dynamics, they always do. People might feel uncertainty, guilt, or even relief, and they'll look to you to make sense of it. Your role is to close the loop honestly, reaffirm shared purpose, and rebuild stability. That might sound like:

"I know transitions can bring mixed feelings. What matters most right now is that we continue supporting each other and stay focused on our shared goals. Priya's contributions helped build this foundation, and now it's our job to carry that forward."

Check in one-on-one with anyone who seemed particularly impacted. Ask how they're doing, not just how the work is going. This is where psychological safety becomes tangible, when people see that your care didn't end when the meeting did.And finally, reflect privately. Ask yourself:

- How did I handle my own emotions in that process?
- What worked well?
- Where could I be clearer next time?

That reflection is what turns a single exit into a lesson that strengthens every future relationship. A study by MIT Sloan found that how organizations handle departures influences future engagement and retention more than pay or perks. When trust is preserved, people feel safe to stay. As I have said, trust is cumulative. Every conversation either deposits or withdraws from it. And the balance you've built is what determines how people experience endings.

Exits as Continuation, Not Closure

Healthy workplaces see exits as a continuation of the relationship, not the end of it.

When the Employee Chooses to Leave

When someone resigns, it can sting, especially if you've poured time and care into them.

But emotionally intelligent leaders resist the impulse to take it personally. "When someone chooses to leave, it's not rejection; it's alignment in action." Celebrate their courage to follow what's right for them. It sends a message to the team that growth is always encouraged, even if it means growing elsewhere.

Stepping-Stone Workplaces

Some organizations, like coffee shops, retailers, or hospitality businesses, attract people at transitional stages of their careers. Even if someone is only with you for a year, your impact can shape their professional DNA. "You may not be someone's forever workplace, but you can still be part of their foundation." When you teach young or temporary employees the value of integrity, communication, and care, those lessons carry through every future team they join. In these workplaces, every employee reflects your organization and can lead to great referrals and positive word of mouth. Be the reason they win in the future!

Filling in the Blanks

- After an exit, silence breeds stories. Fear fills in the blanks left by silence, and fear tells some pretty scary stories. Those stories, whispered in hallways or over coffee, are rarely accurate. Leaders must fill the blanks thoughtfully. Communicate enough to calm uncertainty, but not so much that you compromise confidentiality.Share updates within 24 hours, when possible.
- Keep the message values-based, not personal.
- Reinforce what's constant, the mission, the trust, the path forward.

When you guide the narrative with care and truth, you protect not just reputation, you protect trust.

When You Hold On Too Long

One of the hardest truths in leadership is that keeping someone in a role that no longer fits doesn't serve them or the team. It's tempting to delay a tough conversation out of loyalty, fear, or optimism that "things might turn around." But holding on too long quietly erodes everything you've built.

A 2023 Gallup workplace study found that teams with one consistently low-performing or disengaged member experience a 30% drop in overall productivity and 25% lower morale. The impact isn't limited to output; it spreads emotionally. Colleagues start carrying extra weight, resentment grows, and high performers often disengage to avoid frustration or burnout.

Harvard Business Review reported similar findings: managers who delay necessary staffing changes "create a hidden tax on energy," where up to 40% of their time ends up spent managing tension rather than driving performance. The longer a misalignment lingers, the more trust quietly drains from the system.

When we avoid addressing poor fit, whether in skill, behaviour, or values, the message the rest of the team hears isn't compassion. It's confusion. They start to wonder: Do standards really matter here? And when people lose faith that fairness exists, accountability collapses. Emotionally, it hurts both sides.

The individual you're "protecting" senses the disconnect long before the conversation happens. They feel it in small exclusions, in how projects shift, in the tension that lingers between them and their peers. Instead of protecting them, avoidance prolongs their discomfort and denies them the chance to find alignment elsewhere.

Psychologically safe cultures are not built by avoiding pain; they're built by addressing it with care. True compassion isn't keeping someone comfortable in the wrong place, it's helping them recognize when their best work and best self belong somewhere else. And when you let go with empathy, something powerful happens: trust increases. Not just from the person leaving, but from everyone watching.

As MIT Sloan Management Review summarized in its 2024 *State of Organizational Trust* report, "Transparent and humane exits increase post-turnover engagement among remaining employees by as much as

45%." When handled well, endings reinforce that integrity is real, and that's the ultimate signal of leadership strength.

Reflection & Action: Leading Through Endings

1. **Reflect:** Are you holding on to someone because it's easier than letting go?
2. **Review:** Does your team know what it looks like to leave on a positive note? *(optional: "leave positively" → "leave on a positive note" for slightly smoother phrasing)*
3. **Reinforce:** After a departure, what story will your people tell about how you led?
4. **Rebuild:** What deposits can you make now to strengthen your trust jar for the future?
5. **Remember:** Leadership is about beginnings and endings, both deserve your best self.

When endings are handled with honesty, care, and courage, everyone wins, even if they're no longer on the same team. Trust doesn't stop when the door closes.

That's the real legacy of a happy leader.

Chapter 29
The Sales Mirror

It had been six months since the conversation with Priya.

The team looked and felt different now: lighter, more focused, more connected.

The fog that once lingered over deadlines and confusion had lifted.

Projects were finishing on time, client feedback was glowing, and for the first time in a long while, Alex felt like the team was operating in a rhythm.

They had just wrapped their quarterly results meeting.

Revenue was up by twelve percent.

Employee engagement was at an all-time high.

Even the leadership team had started calling Alex's group "the model team."

But the compliment that struck Alex most came from a client.

After a recent pitch, a long-term customer had said, "Your team just gets us now. It's like you're reading our mind; you don't oversell, you listen, and you make us feel like we're part of something." Alex couldn't stop thinking about that.

Later that week, she was sitting in her office, coffee in hand, scrolling through an email thread about a new account. The conversation between her sales rep, Marco, and the client was seamless, warm, clear, and honest.

Marco hadn't pushed. He'd asked thoughtful questions, paused to listen, and aligned the proposal with what the client had actually said mattered most. It sounded exactly like the conversations Alex had been having with her team. That realization stopped her mid-scroll.

She leaned back in her chair, smiling to herself. *We lead our clients the way we lead our people.* The connection hit her like a light switch turning on.

How the team treated customers was a reflection of how they treated each other. The tone of internal meetings, curious, empathetic, solutions-focused, had started showing up in their external relationships too. Trust, it seemed, had become contagious.

Later that afternoon, Mel dropped by for one of her check-ins. They still spoke regularly, though now the dynamic felt different: less teacher and student, more peers exchanging perspective. Mel leaned against the doorframe. “You look like someone who just solved a mystery.”

Alex laughed. “I think I did. We just had one of our best quarters ever, and I realized something. The way my team sells now, it’s the same way we lead. They’re curious, they listen, they don’t push. They make clients feel understood, not managed.”

Mel smiled knowingly. “That’s emotional intelligence in action. You built a culture inside that now reflects outside. Sales is just leadership with a different audience.”

Alex nodded. “It’s funny; I used to think sales was about persuasion. But it’s really about connection. The same skills we’ve been building; empathy, clarity, self-awareness, they’re what make customers trust us too.”

“Exactly,” Mel said. “Selling and leading aren’t different jobs. They’re both about helping people see possibility and then guiding them there.”

Alex swirled her coffee, thinking. "I guess it's the Everybody Wins method in motion. Take care of your team, they take care of your customers, and the bottom line follows."

Mel grinned. "And that's why you're a happy leader. You've stopped managing transactions. You're leading relationships." Mel winked.

Alex sat quietly for a moment, letting that sink in.

Her mind drifted to an upcoming sales workshop she'd be co-facilitating with Marco. The theme was *The Science and Soul of Selling.*

She smiled at the irony. Six months ago, she'd been the one learning about emotional intelligence. Now she was about to teach it.

Mel stood to leave. "You know," she said, "the best sales cultures are built on the same thing as the best teams: trust and empathy. Maybe that's your next chapter."

Alex nodded, feeling the truth of it settle in. "Yeah," she said, her voice steady. "I think it is."

The next morning, Alex opened a blank slide deck for the upcoming client presentation.

At the top, she typed the title:

"Emotionally Intelligent Sales: Where Leadership Meets Connection."

She smiled. It felt less like a sales strategy and more like a philosophy.

Chapter 30
Emotionally Intelligent Sales

When Alex realized her team's best sales quarter had come from the same behaviours that made them a stronger team, it reframed everything she believed about performance. Sales wasn't a department; it was a mirror of culture. Leaders who create trust internally don't need to "teach" empathy to their salespeople, it's already woven into how they think, listen, and communicate. The customer simply experiences the compounding effect. When leaders ask questions that are curious, their team members tend to ask curious questions as well.

Selling Is Leading

Traditional sales training focuses on scripts, quotas, and closing tactics. Emotionally intelligent selling focuses on curiosity, service, and human connection. We still have goals, and we still ask for the yes, but the map to get to those things looks and feels different. Every customer interaction is a leadership moment. You're guiding someone through uncertainty, building clarity, and inspiring belief, in the product or service, yes, but most importantly, in you.

A 2024 Salesforce study found that 87 percent of buyers now expect sales conversations to be consultative and collaborative, not transactional. The same survey revealed that trustworthiness is the number one driver of repeat business. It's not discounts or features that keep customers; it's how they feel after talking to you, and how they continue to feel after working with you. That's where emotional intelligence shifts from a soft skill to a performance strategy.

Understanding Buyer Desires and Goals

Before Alex could teach her team, the Everybody Wins framework, she wanted them to understand something deeper: customers don't buy products or services; they buy feelings. Every decision a buyer makes is driven by a mix of desire and fear, what they hope to gain and what they're trying to avoid.

Buyer desires are the emotional outcomes: confidence, safety, belonging, growth, pride, relief. Buyer goals are the rational outcomes: saving time, increasing efficiency, improving results, hitting a target.

The emotionally intelligent salesperson, and leader, knows how to connect the two.

When we focus only on logic ("Here are the features, the data, the savings"), we speak to the rational mind. But buying is an emotional act wrapped in logic. People justify decisions with facts but make them with feelings. A 2024 *Harvard Business Review* study found that emotionally connected customers are more than twice as valuable as highly satisfied ones. Connection drives loyalty.

Making the Decision Risk-Free

The second layer of emotional intelligence in sales, and leadership, is reducing perceived risk. At the heart of every buying hesitation is one quiet question:

"What if I'm wrong?"

That same fear shows up inside teams:

"What if I fail?"

"What if I disappoint my boss?"

"What if I can't deliver?"

Emotionally intelligent sellers, like emotionally intelligent leaders, lower that fear by making the next step feel safe. They don't rush the yes; they remove the risk. That might mean offering proof points, testimonials, or data, but more often, it's about offering reassurance:

"If this doesn't deliver the results you expect, we'll make it right."

"Let's start with a pilot so you can test it risk-free."

Inside teams, the same principle applies. When leaders say, "Try it, if it doesn't work, we'll adjust," they activate curiosity instead of anxiety. They build a culture of experimentation instead of perfectionism. Psychologically safe environments are risk-free buying environments. When people trust you, whether they're employees or customers, they stop protecting themselves and start engaging fully.

I like to call this the Safety Sale: the idea that the real close doesn't happen when someone signs the contract, but when they stop feeling afraid. That mindset becomes the foundation for everything that follows.

The Everybody Wins Sales Method

Frameworks are powerful tools for creating structure for sales teams. They provide guardrails while still allowing people the autonomy to connect, be themselves, and create a unique experience for everyone.

Everybody Wins is the overarching framework for the book: create great experiences for your team, and they will create great experiences for your customers. The bottom line will follow, but none of this is possible without taking care of yourself first.

The selling framework itself is a five-step process you can use with your team across different sales environments, whether generating a new lead, holding a first meeting with a prospect, running a sales appointment, or even generating a referral. The same framework applies every time. Ultimately, this is the same framework we've been building throughout the book with our teams as well. (see appendix 14)

Connect Through Energy

Connection begins before the first word is spoken. Customers feel your energy long before they process your pitch. High-EQ leaders know how to regulate emotional tone; they show calm confidence, not performative enthusiasm. They start with presence.

When we talk about the concept of connecting through energy, this is not a subjective idea; this is science. There are reasons why this matters, but ultimately, people can feel someone's confidence, calm, or chaos, and that feeling shapes trust, decisions, and performance.

Emotional Contagion: The Brain-to-Brain Transfer of State

Human beings are wired to synchronize emotionally. Our nervous systems pick up on the emotions of those around us, often in milliseconds, through subtle cues like tone, facial expression, and micro body movements. This process, known as emotional contagion, happens automatically. Studies from the University of Cambridge and the Greater Good Science Center at UC Berkeley show that we unconsciously mimic the facial expressions and postures of others. When we mirror someone's nonverbal cues, our brains release the same neurochemicals they're feeling.

If someone walks into a meeting anxious, their cortisol and adrenaline trigger micro-signals, tense muscles, shallow breathing, and a short tone, that others subconsciously imitate. Within seconds, the whole room feels tighter. Conversely, a calm, grounded leader emits stability. That composure activates oxytocin and dopamine in others, chemicals associated with trust, openness, and motivation. That's why we say energy feels energy, because it does. It's biochemical.

Leadership and sales are both acts of emotional regulation. The most influential person in the room is usually the one whose nervous system stays calmest.

Mirror Neurons: The Empathy Circuit

In the 1990s, neuroscientists in Parma, Italy, discovered mirror neurons, specialized brain cells that fire both when we perform an action and when we observe someone else performing it. These neurons explain empathy on a biological level: our brains don't just see other people's emotions; they simulate them.

When you smile warmly, your client's mirror neurons fire as if they are smiling. When you lean in with genuine curiosity, their brain interprets safety and connection before you've even said a word. A 2022 *Harvard Business Review* article on leadership presence summarized it perfectly:

"Our physiology mirrors the most emotionally dominant nervous system in the room, for better or worse."

That's why high-EQ leaders and sales professionals don't try to control others' energy; they stabilize their own. Their calm becomes contagious.

Neuroception: How the Brain Detects Safety

Dr. Stephen Porges, creator of Polyvagal Theory, introduced the concept of neuroception, the brain's unconscious process of scanning the environment for cues of safety or threat. Before logic, before language, before reason, our nervous system is asking one question:

"Am I safe with you?"

When someone feels unsafe, rushed, pressured, or dismissed, their amygdala (the brain's threat centre) activates, flooding the body with cortisol. This shuts down the prefrontal cortex, the area responsible for reasoning, problem-solving, and decision-making.

That's why high-pressure sales tactics backfire. When we trigger stress, we literally switch off the part of the brain that can say "yes." Conversely, calm, attuned communication signals safety. That activates the parasympathetic nervous system, lowering heart rate, deepening breath, and restoring access to rational thought. In short, people buy when their nervous system relaxes.

This means that when I say "connect through energy," it is ultimately neuroscience in disguise. If you can do the things below, your energies will align (this applies across all steps):

1. **Regulate before you relate.** Take a breath. Get grounded. Your energy sets the emotional thermostat for everyone you speak with.

2. **Lead with calm curiosity.** Curiosity is a neurological cue of safety. It opens the prefrontal cortex and makes people feel seen.

3. **Match and lift.** Mirror the client's tone or pace just enough to connect, then model calm, confident energy to elevate the exchange.

4. **Remember: energy is data.** When someone's tone shifts or body language closes, it's not rejection. it's information. Tune into it, not away from it.

Prioritize the Relationship

People buy from people they trust. They also stay with people who make them feel seen.

In leadership, we call that empathy. In sales, it's attunement. Daniel Pink describes attunement as the ability to "see through another's eyes." When you prioritize relationship over transaction, customers lower their defenses and open up about what truly matters.

Building a relationship in sales is often oversimplified into small talk or friendliness, but true connection goes much deeper, that's attunement. It means tuning into another person's rhythm, emotions, and needs so precisely that they feel understood without needing to explain. It's not about mirroring behaviour to manipulate rapport; it's about aligning your curiosity, pace, and tone with theirs to create genuine psychological safety.

When two people are genuinely engaged, their brains begin to synchronize, a phenomenon called interpersonal neural resonance. Research from Princeton University's Social Neuroscience Lab shows that during deep conversation, listeners' brain waves begin to mirror the speaker's. That neural "mirroring" predicts understanding and empathy more accurately than words alone.

When we're attuned, we notice what isn't being said, the hesitation behind "let me think about it," the energy shift when a topic lands wrong, the spark when something resonates. In emotionally intelligent sales, those moments are data. They tell you where trust is building and where it still needs to grow.

This is why rapport isn't built through charm; it's built through presence. True rapport happens when a customer feels, "*You see me. You're not trying to sell to me; you're trying to understand me.*" That's when the human brain releases oxytocin, the neurochemical of connection, and defenses lower. The nervous system relaxes, making collaboration possible.

Trust, in this context, is cumulative. It's built in micro-moments: remembering something they said last week, following up when you promised, listening longer than is comfortable. It's consistency over charm. Because in the end, the foundation of sales and the foundation of leadership are the same, people want to be seen, heard, and valued. And attunement is how you make that happen.

Understand Their Needs

Understanding someone's needs is not about running through a checklist of questions; it's about learning who they are, what they value, and what's driving their decisions beneath the surface. In emotionally intelligent sales, discovery is the art of listening between the lines. It's hearing both the words that are spoken and the meaning that lives underneath them.

Most people communicate on two levels: the rational and the emotional. The rational answers tell you what they need: a faster system, a better outcome, a lower cost.

The emotional answers tell you why they need it: recognition, security, relief, belonging, or growth. When you're truly listening, you'll start to hear the difference. You'll notice the pause before they mention a past frustration, the shift in tone when they talk about a goal that matters, the spark when they describe success in their own words. That's not small talk; that's insight.

The emotionally intelligent communicator uses discovery to build understanding that goes far beyond features and benefits. They connect curiosity with empathy to uncover the emotional drivers behind decisions, the deep motivators that influence behaviour.

A 2024 Harvard study on decision science found that 95% of purchasing decisions are made subconsciously, guided by emotional context rather than logic. People may say they're buying efficiency, but what they're really buying is peace of mind. They may say they want innovation, but what they're seeking is recognition, the feeling of being seen as forward-thinking or successful.

To understand someone's needs is to ask questions that reveal those layers.

Questions like:

- "What would success look like for you personally?"
- "When this is solved, what changes for you?"
- "What would make this feel effortless?"
- "If this didn't work, what would worry you most?"

These questions create space for reflection. They slow the conversation down just enough for truth to emerge. And as people articulate what truly matters, they begin to feel seen. and that is where trust begins to deepen.

Great discovery conversations don't just identify gaps; they reveal goals, fears, and aspirations. They allow you to design solutions that don't just meet expectations, they exceed them, because they address the deeper win: the emotional outcome that defines what success feels like for that person.

When you master discovery, you move from problem-solver to partner. You stop guessing what matters and start knowing, and that knowledge is what transforms every conversation from a transaction into a relationship.

Exceed Expectations

Exceeding expectations isn't about doing more; it's about doing what matters more.

It's not volume; it's value. When we truly understand what drives a person, their emotional motivators, their version of success, their unspoken fears, we can design solutions that make them feel seen, supported, and successful.

In traditional sales, exceeding expectations is often framed as surprise-and-delight moments or over-delivering. In emotionally intelligent sales, it's about precision: tailoring your solution so that it resonates with what someone values most. This is where leadership and sales completely overlap; both are about helping others win.

You exceed expectations when you connect your product, service, or idea directly to the outcomes your customer cares about and the emotions they want to feel. It's not about giving them more; it's about giving them what they truly need.

That means translating discovery into design. If they value efficiency, your solution should save time and make them feel in control. If they value recognition, your solution should give them something they'll be proud to share. If they value belonging, your approach should make them feel like they're part of something bigger.

When leaders or sales professionals deliver this kind of emotional precision, clients don't just see results, they feel them.

The Emotional ROI of Exceeding Expectations

Research from Gallup's *2024 State of the Customer Report* found that clients who feel emotionally supported during the sales process are 3.2 times more likely to repurchase and 4.6 times more likely to recommend the organization to others. Why? Because emotion creates memory.

People don't remember what you said; they remember how you made them feel while solving their problem. That's the emotional return on investment: the feeling of confidence, clarity, or relief that makes someone say, "I trust them."

Every time you deliver in a way that connects to those emotional needs, you're making a trust deposit, one that compounds over time. And just like leadership, those deposits build loyalty that lasts far beyond a single transaction.

Designing the "Deeper Win"

To exceed expectations, you have to think beyond the surface-level problem. Every product or service you offer solves a functional need. The deeper win solves an emotional need.

Ask yourself:

- What does success look like for them, not the organization, not the metrics, but the person?
- How can I make this solution easier, faster, or more meaningful?
- What would make them feel proud to have chosen this?

The best solutions are co-created. When you involve your customer in the design, asking, clarifying, adjusting, they feel ownership of the outcome. That ownership is where advocacy is born.

Exceeding expectations transforms the dynamic from seller and buyer to partners in success. That's why emotionally intelligent sellers don't chase one-time wins; they build systems of trust. They measure success not by closed deals, but by ongoing relationships.

When people feel understood and supported, they stop shopping for alternatives because they've already found someone who sees them. That's what *Everybody Wins* really means: your customers win through clarity, your team wins through connection, and your business wins through loyalty.

5. Ask for the Sale

By the time you reach the point of asking for the sale, the decision is rarely about price or product; it's about trust, or at least it should be.

When you've connected with genuine energy, built relationship through attunement, and understood what truly matters, asking for the sale is simply the natural next step.

It's not pressure. It's partnership.

The most confident asks come from leaders who are grounded, not from hype or force, but from emotional alignment. Confidence is energy. When you believe in what you're offering, people feel it.

That's why regulating your energy before the ask is so critical. Take a breath. Centre yourself. Ask from a place of calm rather than urgency or fear. Because your nervous system speaks before your mouth does, and if you're anxious, they'll sense it.

An emotionally intelligent ask might sound like:

"Based on what you've shared and what we've discussed, I believe this solution fits what success looks like for you. Are you ready for us to move forward together?"

It's confident, collaborative, and respectful of autonomy. It invites a yes without demanding it.

Objections: Clarity, Not Conflict

When someone hesitates or pushes back, it's rarely rejection; it's protection. Objections are emotional data points, revealing where fear or uncertainty still lives.

The emotionally intelligent professional doesn't counter objections; they clarify them.

They listen for what's underneath:

- Is it a fear of making the wrong decision, or failing?
- Is it about timing, trust, or understanding value?
- Is it a signal that we missed a deeper need earlier in the process?

The best objection handling isn't defensive; it's discovery 2.0. It's looping back to the "Understand and Exceed Needs" phases with new insight and empathy.

You might say:

"It sounds like you're concerned about X. Can you tell me more about that?"

"That's a fair point. Let's revisit what's most important to you and make sure this still aligns."

When you handle objections this way, you're not rescuing the sale; you're reinforcing trust.

Leading Emotionally Intelligent Sales Teams

Everything in this model scales from individual conversations to entire organizations.

Teaching emotional intelligence in sales isn't about replacing metrics; it's about redefining what they mean. Too many teams measure performance through volume: how many calls were made, how many emails were sent, how many deals were closed. But quantity doesn't create loyalty. Connection does.

Leaders who drive sustained sales success focus less on how often their teams reach out and more on how well they connect. They coach curiosity, listening, empathy, and follow-through. They review conversations not just for closing techniques, but for tone, pacing, and alignment with customer values.

An emotionally intelligent sales culture rewards:

- Curiosity over compliance
- Listening over talking
- Clarity over pressure
- Trust over transactions

When leaders develop these qualities, performance naturally follows. The numbers improve, not because people are being pushed, but because they're proud of how they sell. That's the difference between managing performance and leading excellence.

Sales is simply leadership with a customer on the other end of the conversation. And when leaders create a culture that values emotional intelligence as much as skill, everybody wins; the team, the customer, and the organization.

Reflection & Action: Leading the Emotionally Intelligent Sale

1. **Regulate Your Energy**

   Before your next client or stakeholder conversation, take 60 seconds to centre yourself. What emotional signal are you sending when you walk in: calm confidence or anxious urgency? Remember, your nervous system sets the tone before your words ever do.

2. **Listen Between the Lines**

   After each conversation, reflect: Did I truly listen, not just to what was said, but to what wasn't? What emotions, needs, or motivations surfaced beneath the surface story?

3. **Design for Connection, Not Just Convenience**

   Review one customer or team touchpoint. Is it built to make things faster, or to make people feel valued? Where can you add a moment of genuine human connection?

4. **Ask With Confidence and Care**

   Whether it's a sale, a proposal, or a team commitment, notice how you ask.

   Are you asking from alignment and belief, or from pressure and fear?

Confidence is energy, and care is how you make it safe for others to say yes.

5. **Coach for Quality, Not Quantity**

   As a leader, look at how you measure success on your team. Are you counting calls, or cultivating conversations? Shift your coaching to focus on curiosity, trust, and the emotional experience you're creating, because that's what drives sustainable performance.

Remember: Every Interaction Is Leadership

Every time you connect, you're leading, whether it's a client, a colleague, or a direct report. People remember how you make them feel far longer than what you make them do. That's your true brand and your lasting legacy.

Chapter 31
Building the Bridges

The morning sunlight spilled across the office, catching the corner of Alex's whiteboard. It was covered with arrows, names, and notes, the visual map of her world. Sales connected to Service. Service to Operations. Operations to Marketing. And somehow, everyone connected to her.

Alex smiled at the mess. It wasn't chaos anymore; it was clarity. For the first time, she could see the bigger picture.

Over the past few months, her team had changed. They were clearer, calmer, and more confident. Expectations were no longer vague; accountability didn't feel like confrontation. The shift was showing up everywhere, in the way meetings started on time, how ideas were shared, and how laughter had replaced tension. But lately, something new had been bubbling up. It started when John from Marketing stopped by her office.

"Hey, I wanted to ask: how does your team decide which client requests to prioritize? We're trying to align messaging, but sometimes it feels like we're chasing different goals."

Alex blinked. "You know what, John? That's a fair question."

Then it happened again. Ibukun called to talk through a bottleneck. "We're not broken," she said, "but we're not totally in sync either. It's like everyone's rowing hard, but in slightly different directions."

That night, Alex sat at her kitchen table, coffee in hand, thinking about what Mel had told her months ago: *Leadership doesn't stop at your team. It's how you help the system work better for everyone.*

She realized she'd been so focused on her team's rhythm that she hadn't noticed how disconnected the departments around them felt. They weren't fighting; they were simply unaligned. Each group was doing their best, but they were operating with different assumptions, different priorities, and sometimes even different definitions of success.

Alex decided to do what had always worked best: start with curiosity.

The next morning, she pulled together a meeting. Not a presentation, but a conversation. Representatives from every department were invited: Sales, Service, Marketing, Operations, Finance.

They came in expecting a standard agenda. Instead, Alex handed everyone a sticky note.

"Write down one thing your team needs from another department to make your job easier," she said. "And one thing you think they need from you."

The room went quiet. Then pens started moving. Within minutes, the walls were covered in colour, patterns of expectations, frustrations, and wishes that had never been said out loud.

Jamie, her team lead, pointed to one note. "Marketing doesn't know when we change delivery timelines." John nodded. "Because Operations doesn't always tell us first."

Ibukun added, "And Operations doesn't know until Finance releases approvals."

They all laughed, not in mockery, but in relief.

"It's not that we're bad at communication," Alex said. "It's that we've been communicating inside our own walls."

She grabbed a marker and drew circles on the whiteboard, overlapping, intersecting, and connecting. "Each of us holds a piece of the whole," she said. "But the only way the system works is if the space between us does too."

As the conversation unfolded, Alex could feel the principles of emotional intelligence at work. Self-awareness in leaders who admitted what they didn't know. Empathy in teams who started listening without defensiveness. Reality testing as they compared assumptions to facts. And impulse control as people paused before reacting, something that hadn't always come easy.

By the end of the meeting, they had a shared list of what "working well together" meant:

- Clear timelines.
- Consistent updates.
- Defined decision points.
- And a commitment to revisit, not just react.

Alex looked around the room. People who had once only spoken through email threads were now debating ideas face-to-face. The walls that had once divided departments were now filled with bridges made of sticky notes.

That evening, she called Mel. "How's it going, bridge builder?" Mel teased.

Alex laughed. "Better than expected. Turns out most of our issues weren't in the people; they were in the spaces between them."

Mel's voice softened. "That's where leadership lives, Alex. Not above people, not ahead of them, *between* them. You've learned to lead across, not just down."

Alex smiled, looking at the now-empty meeting room, the whiteboard still covered in bright colours, proof that something had shifted.

For the first time, she could see what was next. Not a new system. Not another policy.

But a culture where emotional intelligence wasn't just a leadership skill; it was the operating system of the entire organization.

Chapter 32
Leading with Emotional Intelligence: The Culture Multiplier

Leadership isn't a role; it's a rhythm. Every time a leader communicates, recognizes, or redirects, they send cues that either amplify or drain performance. Emotional intelligence turns those micro-moments into momentum.

There is neuroscience to winning. The human brain is wired to pursue progress. Each time we achieve something, checking a task off a list, hitting a target, receiving recognition, the brain releases dopamine, the neurotransmitter of motivation and reward. In high-trust, emotionally intelligent workplaces, leaders understand this chemistry. They design experiences that create frequent, authentic wins; not just end-of-quarter celebrations, but daily signals of progress and purpose.

When people know how to win, their motivation becomes self-sustaining. A 2023 Gallup meta-analysis found that employees who can clearly describe what success looks like for them are 4.6 times more likely to be engaged at work. It's not about trophies; it's about clarity, feedback, and belonging.

Energy as the New Performance Metric

Traditional performance systems measure output. Emotionally intelligent cultures measure energy flow **and** results.

- **Mental energy:** clarity of goals and autonomy in how to achieve them.
- **Emotional energy:** trust and psychological safety to speak up and learn.

- **Spiritual energy:** connection to purpose, the "why" behind the work.
- **Physical energy:** sustainable pace, rest, and renewal.

When leaders manage these four systems intentionally, performance rises because the brain and body are aligned with the mission. Neuroscience shows that sustained high performance depends less on pressure and more on psychological recovery between demands. EQ-driven leaders know when to push and when to pause.

From Compliance to Commitment

Rules create compliance; empathy creates commitment. An emotionally intelligent organization translates expectations into shared meaning. HR policies become promises of fairness. Operational processes become guardrails that protect focus. Change initiatives become stories of growth rather than fear. When people feel seen and supported, discretionary effort, the extra energy people choose to give, skyrockets. According to a 2024 MIT Sloan study, employees who rate their leaders high in empathy deliver 32 percent higher individual productivity and reduce voluntary turnover by 60 percent.

EQ in Action Across the Organization

Emotional intelligence isn't a "soft skill" that lives in HR or leadership retreats. It's the operating system that drives every function in a healthy, high-performing organization. When EQ becomes embedded across departments, the organization stops running on rules and starts running on relationships.

Human Resources

Policies tell your people what you value most. In a low-EQ environment, HR becomes the compliance department, writing rules to prevent problems. In an emotionally intelligent culture, HR becomes the energy department, designing experiences that protect people while helping them grow.

Before writing or revising a policy, pause and ask:

- How will this make people feel?
- What problem are we trying to prevent, and what trust might we unintentionally break?
- Does this policy assume the best in people or protect us from the worst?

When HR uses empathy as its lens, policies feel fair because they are rooted in understanding. They communicate belonging instead of bureaucracy.

Operations

Operations is the heartbeat of consistency. Processes can either free people or frustrate them, and EQ determines which. Emotionally intelligent operations design systems that make expectations clear without stripping away autonomy. Involve the people who use the process to help shape it.

Ask:

- Where do you lose time or energy in your day?
- What steps could we simplify without losing quality?
- What part of this system makes your job easier, and what makes it harder?

When employees help design the systems they live in, ownership replaces compliance.

Clarity becomes confidence, and confidence drives consistency.

Finance

Budgets are moral documents; they reveal what an organization truly values.

An emotionally intelligent finance team understands that every line item represents a human decision. Instead of asking, "What can we cut?" EQ-minded finance leaders ask, "What are we investing in?"

Questions that guide emotionally intelligent budgeting:

- Does this spending align with our stated values?
- How does this decision impact the people delivering or receiving the work?
- Are we optimizing for short-term savings or long-term sustainability?

When numbers are grounded in empathy, money becomes a message of trust, proof that people and purpose are both priorities.

Change Management

Change is emotional before it's operational. People don't resist change; they resist uncertainty. Emotionally intelligent change leaders build safety through transparency and empathy, helping people see themselves in the story of transformation.

In any transition, leaders can ask:

- What might this change feel like to someone who didn't choose it?
- How can we make progress visible so people know it's working?
- What fears might go unspoken, and how can we address them openly?

By naming emotions early, leaders reduce resistance later. Trust grows not from perfection, but from honest conversations about imperfection.

Customer Experience

Customers are not data points; they are humans navigating their own pressures, needs, and hopes. Emotional intelligence turns service into partnership by teaching teams to listen between the lines. A complaint isn't conflict; it's communication. A thank-you isn't closure; it's connection.

EQ-guided customer teams ask:

- What emotion is driving this customer's behaviour right now?
- How do we make them feel seen, not sold to?
- What story will they tell about us after this interaction?

When empathy guides experience, customers stop being buyers; they become believers.

The Performance Equation

Performance = Energy × Clarity × Trust

Pressure without clarity breeds burnout. Clarity without energy creates apathy. Trust without accountability stalls progress. When all three multiply, people feel safe enough to stretch, and that's where innovation lives.

When every department operates with emotional intelligence, performance stops depending on individual heroics. It becomes systemic, built into how people think, talk, and decide. That's when culture becomes a multiplier.

Chapter 33
The Happy Leader Legacy

The morning sunlight streamed across the boardroom table as Alex looked around at her team. There were new faces now, and a few missing ones too. Change was normal here now. Expected, even. Healthy. A lot of the change was related to others' growth and success in new roles within the organization, some leading their own teams now.

What had once been a tense, uncertain department had become a confident, connected team. They didn't always agree, but they always spoke up. They didn't always win, but they always learned.

Alex took a slow breath as her leadership team presented updates, clear, concise, and energized. It wasn't perfect. But it was real. There was laughter, problem-solving, a few awkward pauses, and even a shared eye-roll when technology lagged. But there was also something that hadn't been there before: trust.

Later that day, she met with Jordan, one of her newer managers. Jordan had joined six months ago and was proving to be both ambitious and curious, a mix Alex recognized from her own early days. They sat down in her office for their regular one-on-one.

Jordan started, "I wanted to talk about team morale. They're performing well, but something feels... off. I can't quite name it." Alex smiled. "You don't need to fix it yet. You just need to feel it. That's leadership. It's sensing energy before you have evidence."

Jordan laughed softly. "That's not in any of the management books." "Neither was most of what I learned," Alex said. They talked for a while about the team's dynamic, the mix of personalities, the subtle tension between speed and quality, and the quiet burnout that can hide beneath great results. When Jordan left, Alex felt that familiar mix of pride and nostalgia, watching someone else take steps she'd once stumbled through.

That afternoon, she sat at her desk, jotting notes for the upcoming quarterly meeting. On her screen, she wrote the theme: "Everybody Wins: A Year of Growth and Gratitude."

As she typed, she thought of Mel. She hadn't spoken to her mentor in a couple of months, but she still heard her voice in small moments: the calm reminders, the reframes, the gentle pushes toward courage. Alex sent Mel a quick text, just to say she was thinking of her and that they needed coffee soon.

Alex opened her journal and wrote:

Be your best self, so you can build great relationships.

Help others "live happy," and everybody wins.

It wasn't a slogan anymore. It was a truth. A way of operating. A culture that would keep evolving, with or without her.

She looked out the window at her team laughing around the coffee bar. Their energy filled the space. And for the first time, Alex didn't feel like she was carrying them. They were carrying each other.

Chapter 34
Helping Others Live Happy (Reflection)

Leadership isn't a ladder to climb; it's a circle you keep expanding. Every time you invest in your people, you extend that circle. Every time you create clarity, empathy, or trust, you widen it again. That's how culture grows, one intentional moment at a time.

The Formula for Legacy

Every part of The Happy Leader Method comes full circle here, a cycle that starts within you and spreads outward through every relationship, every decision, and every moment of courage.

1. **Be Your Best Self - Manage your energy and mindset.**

It all begins here. With you. You can't create clarity when your mind is cluttered. You can't build calm when your energy is scattered. You can't inspire belief in others when you've forgotten how to believe in yourself.

Being your best self isn't about perfection; it's about presence. It's about recognizing when your energy is low, when your perspective has narrowed, or when your inner critic has grown louder than your purpose.

Leaders who manage their energy model sustainability. They show that success doesn't have to cost you your health, your peace, or your joy. They prove that strength and softness can coexist, that rest is not a reward, it's a requirement. When you're at your best, people don't just see it; they feel it. Your steadiness becomes their safety. Your optimism becomes their courage. That's where leadership starts.

2. **Build Great Relationships - Create trust through empathy, consistency, and care.**

No strategy succeeds without relationships. The best leaders don't just manage people; they connect with them. They listen with intent. They notice the pause before someone speaks, the tone that changes mid-sentence, and the courage it takes to bring forward a hard truth. Empathy isn't just a skill; it's an act of leadership. Consistency isn't just a process; it's a promise. Care isn't a soft word; it's the strongest foundation you can build on.

Relationships are the infrastructure of success. They carry people through change, pressure, and uncertainty. When trust is high, teams move faster, communicate more clearly, and solve bigger problems together. When people know they are seen and supported, they don't just perform for you; they believe *with* you.

3. **Everybody Wins - Align personal goals with organizational purpose.**

Work is at its best when people can see how their individual success contributes to something bigger than themselves. "Everybody Wins" isn't just a slogan; it's a leadership mindset. It's understanding that when the team wins, the customer wins. When the customer wins, the company wins. And when the company wins, everyone feels proud of the part they played.

Leaders who practice this alignment make winning visible. They celebrate progress, not just perfection. They help their people understand what success looks like and why it matters. When people know how to win, they stay. When they stay, trust deepens. And when trust deepens, performance soars. That's how momentum becomes culture.

4. **Help Others Live Happy - Lift others by helping them find their own clarity, confidence, and purpose.**

This is the heart of legacy. Helping others live happy means caring enough to develop them, not just for the role they're in, but for the life they're building. It means creating space for people to discover their strengths, name their goals, and stretch into the best versions of themselves.

It means being the kind of leader who doesn't need the spotlight because your greatest achievement is watching others shine. When you help others live happy, your influence outlives your title. The lessons you've modelled, about balance, trust, and growth, echo long after you've left the room.

Legacy isn't about tenure or titles. It's about the energy you leave behind: the belief that people can do hard things, that kindness and accountability can coexist, and that happiness and success are not opposites but partners.

That's what makes a Happy Leader.

These steps are not sequential; they're cyclical. There will be times when you feel like you're right back at the beginning, refocusing on energy, rebuilding trust, or redefining what success means. That's not failure. That's leadership.

The best leaders don't move in straight lines. They evolve, recalibrate, and grow in spirals, expanding outward as they deepen within.

The Legacy of Energy

Culture isn't a document. It's the invisible current that runs through conversations, decisions, and how people treat one another on the hardest days. Energy is legacy. When a leader consistently brings clarity instead of confusion, calm instead of chaos, and belief instead of blame, that energy outlasts them. It lives in how people speak to new hires, how meetings feel, and how decisions are made when no one is watching. That's how leaders have an impact on every relationship they have within an organization.

The happiest workplaces are not families; they're partnerships. Both sides bring something valuable to the table: the organization offers purpose and opportunity; the employee offers energy and effort. When both invest intentionally, the return is exponential. Leaders help their people understand the "why" behind the work. Employees take ownership of how they show up. Together, they co-create a place where people want to belong and where success feels shared.

That's how you build a legacy that lasts.

Reflection & Action: Living the Circle

1. **Revisit Your Energy.** What fills your tank, and what drains it? Schedule recovery as deliberately as you schedule results.
2. **Reassess Your Relationships.** Who needs more clarity, support, or feedback from you right now?
3. **Realign the Wins.** Are your team's definitions of success still matching the organization's needs?
4. **Redefine Your Role.** Are you mentoring others to lead with the same balance of care and accountability?
5. **Remember the Circle.** Leadership isn't about arriving; it's about returning. Return to your best self. Return to connection. Return to purpose.

Because when you help others live happy, you don't just build a stronger business; you build a better world.

Let's Keep the Conversation Going

If you've made it here, thank you, truly. You've spent time reflecting, questioning, and maybe even rethinking what leadership means to you. That's the work. And it never really ends.

The Happy Leader isn't meant to be a one-time read; it's a companion for the moments when you need to reset, re-centre, or remember why you started. My hope is that these pages reminded you that leadership is human work, emotional, imperfect, and deeply worth it.

As you go back to your teams, your meetings, and your life, keep practising what we've explored together: Be your best self. Build great relationships. Help others win.

And whenever you can, help others live happy.

If something in this book sparked an idea, a question, or a story, I'd love to hear it. Connection is where growth happens. You can always find me sharing insights, announcing upcoming sessions, and having conversations about leadership, emotional intelligence, and workplace culture on my professional platforms. Whether it's a keynote, a workshop, or a simple message, the goal is the same: to keep learning, leading, sharing, growing, and lifting others up together.

Because learning doesn't stop when the book ends. It continues in every conversation, every act of courage, and every choice to lead with care.

Thank you for being part of this journey. Keep going, and keep helping others live happy.

, *Melissa Maloney*

Appendix List

Appendix 1:

4 Energy Systems Self-Assessment

Your energy fuels everything - your clarity, your decisions, your relationships, your leadership.

This assessment helps you understand where your energy is strongest, where it drains fastest, and where small shifts can create big results.

You'll rate yourself across four systems:

1. Physical Energy (Rest and Movement)
2. Mental Energy (Prioritization and Focus)
3. Emotional Energy (Safety and Trust)
4. Spiritual Energy (Purpose and Meaning)

These systems do not operate in isolation. They influence each other. When one is depleted, the others must compensate, and performance suffers. This tool helps you see the patterns so you can lead with intention.

PART 1 - ENERGY SELF-ASSESSMENT (SCORING)

Instructions:

Read each statement and rate how true it is for you in a typical week.

Scale:

1 = Never true

2 = Rarely true

3 = Sometimes true

4 = Often true

5 = Almost always true

A. PHYSICAL ENERGY (10 items)

1. I wake up feeling rested most days.
2. I'm able to maintain energy throughout my workday without relying on caffeine or adrenaline.
3. I move my body regularly (walks, stretching, exercise).
4. I nourish myself with food that supports my energy, not drains it.
5. I take breaks before I'm exhausted.
6. I can physically feel when I'm depleted and know what helps me recover.
7. I rarely work through lunch or skip meals.
8. My sleep routine is consistent.
9. I feel physically capable of handling my workload.
10. I have the stamina to be present with my team and my family/friends after work.

Subtotal: ___ / 50

B. MENTAL ENERGY (10 items)

1. I can focus on one task at a time without constant distraction.
2. I set priorities intentionally rather than reacting to everything that comes in.
3. I have systems that support my clarity (calendars, lists, workflows).

4. I make decisions without overthinking or spiraling mentally.
5. I can quiet mental noise when needed.
6. I reduce unnecessary notifications and interruptions.
7. I rarely feel overwhelmed by competing demands.
8. I use time intentionally rather than reactively.
9. I start my day with clarity instead of chaos.
10. I can "turn off" my brain enough to rest or be present.

Subtotal: ___ / 50

C. EMOTIONAL ENERGY (10 items)

1. I can name my emotions as they show up.
2. I regulate my reactions instead of reacting impulsively.
3. I trust and feel safe in the relationships I have at work.
4. I'm not easily thrown off by others' moods.
5. I listen fully to others without planning my rebuttal.
6. I can handle difficult conversations respectfully and calmly.
7. I don't personalize feedback or conflict.
8. I feel connected to the people I lead.
9. I have people I can talk to about challenges.
10. I feel safe to be myself at work.

Subtotal: ___ / 50

D. SPIRITUAL ENERGY (10 items)

This system is not about religion, it is about purpose, meaning, alignment, and the "why" behind your effort.

1. I feel connected to a sense of purpose in my work.
2. I make decisions that align with my values.
3. I feel that my work matters.
4. I have clarity around what I'm trying to build or contribute to.
5. I rarely feel like I'm "just going through the motions."
6. I can find meaning even in stressful seasons.
7. I feel connected to something bigger than myself, people, purpose, or impact.
8. I'm proud of how I show up.
9. I know what "winning" looks like for my life and leadership.
10. I make space to reflect on what's important.

Subtotal: ___ / 50

PART 2 — SCORING & INTERPRETATION

Add your totals from each section:

- Physical Energy: _____ / 50
- Mental Energy: _____ / 50
- Emotional Energy: _____ / 50
- Spiritual Energy: _____ / 50

Interpreting Each System

40–50 = High Energy Availability

You have strong habits, clear awareness, and supportive routines. Your energy flows easily and fuels your leadership.

25–39 = Moderate Energy

This system works... until it doesn't.

You have solid habits but also drains that you may be ignoring.

Small shifts will create big differences.

10–24 = Low Energy

This system is costing you.

It is likely affecting other systems too.

This is your highest-impact area for improvement.

Check all that apply:

- □ High emotional + low physical → burnout risk
- □ High mental + low spiritual → productivity without meaning
- □ High spiritual + low mental → inspired but scattered
- □ High physical + low emotional → productive but disconnected
- □ Low in 3 or 4 systems → chronic depletion

Each pattern has leadership consequences, and opportunities.

Appendix 2:

Time Tracking Activity Chart

For the next week:

1. Track your time: Write down what you're doing in 30–60-minute blocks.
2. Mark each task: "E" for Energizing, "D" for Draining, "T" for Time Waster.
3. Review patterns: What percentage of your time is spent in energizing activities? What can you delegate, drop, or streamline?
4. Choose one change: Identify one small shift that will increase your energy by at least 1 percent next week.

Sample Tracking Sheet

Activity	"E", "D", or "T"	Small Shift/ Strategy to change if needed

Appendix 3:

Time Management Matrix

Adapted from Steven Covey's The 7 Habits of Highly Effective People

Quadrant 1: Urgent + Important	Quadrant 2: Not Urgent + Important
Crises, deadlines, problems that can't wait.	Relationship-building, planning, skill development, prevention, strategy.
Quadrant 3: Urgent + Not Important	**Quadrant 4:** Not Urgent + Not Important
Interruptions, some emails, most meetings, other people's "emergencies."	Timewasters, mindless scrolling, busywork.

Appendix 4:

The Culture Blueprint

A practical worksheet for designing the culture your team lives, feels, and performs within.

Culture is not what you say, it's what you repeat. This blueprint gives leaders a simple, actionable framework to intentionally design the culture they want their team to experience every day. Use it during onboarding, team resets, performance alignment, strategy planning, or anytime you want to strengthen trust and clarity.

HOW TO USE THIS TOOL

1. Complete the blueprint yourself.
2. Share it with your team.
3. Co-create: invite their input, feedback, and examples.
4. Revisit quarterly, culture evolves as your team does.

This becomes your shared language.

Your team's manual.

Your consistency anchor.

SECTION 1: LEADER IDENTITY

"Your team deserves to know how you lead."

Use this section to describe the type of leader you strive to be and what people can expect from you on a daily basis.

A. What I Value as a Leader

(Examples: consistency, transparency, being direct and caring, clarity before speed)

My leadership values:

B. How I Communicate

This sets expectations and reduces uncertainty, one of the biggest sources of employee stress.

- How I give feedback:

- What I mean when I say "urgent":

- How I celebrate wins:

- How I address misalignment:

- What I need from my team:

C. My Care & Credibility Practices

These are the small, intentional actions your team can count on you for, the ones that build trust and psychological safety.

Examples:

- I close loops.
- I follow through on commitments.

- I check in, not check up.
- I will always be honest with you, even if it's hard.
- I will never let you be surprised by feedback.

My trust-building commitments:

____

____

____

SECTION 2: VALUES IN ACTION

"Values aren't posters. They're behaviours."

Most organizations have values. Few define what those values look like in real life.

Use this template to translate abstract values into observable behaviours.

Value #1: ____

This looks like:

- ____
- ____

This does NOT look like:

- ____
- ____

Value #2: ____

This looks like:

- ____
- ____

This does NOT look like:

- ____
- ____

Value #3: ____________________________________

This looks like:

- ____
- ____

This does NOT look like:

- ____
- ____

SECTION 3: COMMUNICATION NORMS

"Communication is the culture."

Define how communication happens on your team so people don't waste energy guessing:

Our Team's Communication Agreements

- How we share updates:

- How we make decisions (Leaf/Branch/Root):
- How we close communication loops:
- How we ask questions or raise concerns:
- How we respond to conflict or misalignment:

Meeting Norms

- Meeting purpose clarity
- Start and end on time
- Agenda sent ahead
- Recap includes Results, Rules, Roles
- Space for candor

(Write team-specific norms below.)

SECTION 4: PSYCHOLOGICAL SAFETY PRACTICES

"Safety fuels performance."

Psychological safety is built through consistency, transparency, and authenticity - and protected through everyday rituals.

Our Team Safety Practices

Check all that apply or add your own:

□ We normalize mistakes as part of growth

□ We ask curiosity-first questions ("What got in the way?")

□ We acknowledge feelings before solutions

□ We give feedback early, not all at once

□ We celebrate learning, not just outcomes

□ We practice Above-the-Line thinking

What safety looks like on our team:

____

____

What safety does NOT look like:

____

____

____

SECTION 5: ACTION TO ALIGNMENT

"Clarity today prevents conflict tomorrow."

This section connects expectations accountability ownership.

Use it to define your rules of engagement:

A. Our Team's Alignment Commitments

- We clarify Results, Rules, and Roles before beginning work.
- We repeat back what we heard to confirm alignment.
- We tell the truth kindly and quickly.
- We use candor to care for each other.
- We repair trust when it breaks.

Add your team's own alignment principles:

____

____

B. Our Team's Accountability Agreements

Accountability = support + alignment.

Write your commitments:

- How we stay aligned: ____________________________
- How we reset after missteps: _______________________
- How we ensure nobody is surprised by feedback:

  ____
- How we hold ourselves accountable:

  ____

SECTION 6: CULTURE PULSE CHECK (Quarterly)

Use these prompts to keep your culture alive and intentional.

1. Where are we strongest right now as a team?
2. Where is energy leaking?
3. Where is clarity missing?
4. What expectations need to be refreshed?
5. Who needs support?
6. What do we want to celebrate more?
7. What do we want to shift moving forward?

This becomes your north star, your foundational document. Revisit it. Share it. Use it.

When culture is intentional, clarity is easy. When clarity is easy, everybody wins.

Appendix 5:

Why / What I'll Do / What I Don't Know / When We'll Revisit

A clarity tool for leaders and teams to prevent confusion, assumptions, and drift.

Use this framework anytime you're setting a new expectation, clarifying a deliverable, planning a transition, assigning ownership, or moving through change.

It ensures that no one leaves a conversation filling in the blanks.

1. WHY: THE PURPOSE

Why does this matter? What outcome are we aiming for? Explain the reason behind the work, expectation, or decision. People commit more fully when they understand the purpose.

Example prompts:

"The reason we're doing this is..."

"This supports our goal of..."

"The impact of this is..."

Write your WHY:

____

____

____

2. WHAT I'LL DO: THE ACTIONS & COMMITMENTS

What exactly will I take responsibility for? Define clear, observable steps. This strengthens trust and alignment.

Example prompts:

"Here's what I will deliver..."

"Here is my part of the process..."

"Here is what I'm committing to do next..."

My commitments:

____

____

____

3. WHAT I DON'T KNOW: OPEN QUESTIONS & DEPENDENCIES

What information, clarity, or resources do I still need? Naming uncertainty prevents assumptions and encourages honest dialogue. This is where psychological safety expands.

Example prompts:

"Here is what I'm unclear about..."

"I need clarification on..."

"I'm unsure how to proceed with..."

My open questions:

____

4. WHEN WE'LL REVISIT: CHECKPOINT & ACCOUNTABILITY

When will we review progress, adjust, or realign? Accountability is not pressure, it's alignment.

Example prompts:

"Let's check in on..."

"We'll revisit this after..."

"Our follow-up meeting will be..."

Next checkpoint:

___

It creates clarity through transparency and prevents the "I thought you meant..." gaps that erode trust.

Appendix 6:

Decision Tree Image

Please note: This concept was written by Susan Scott in her book ***Fierce Conversations: Achieving Success at Work and in Life One Conversation at a Time.***

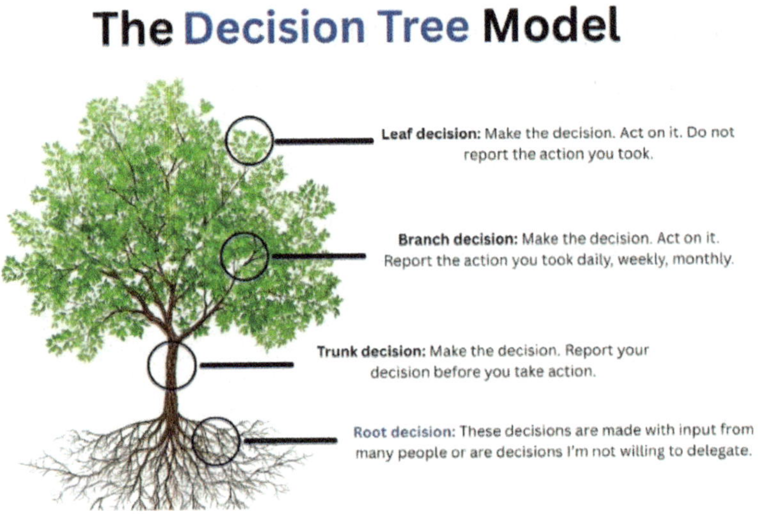

Appendix 7:

EQ Drive Matrix:

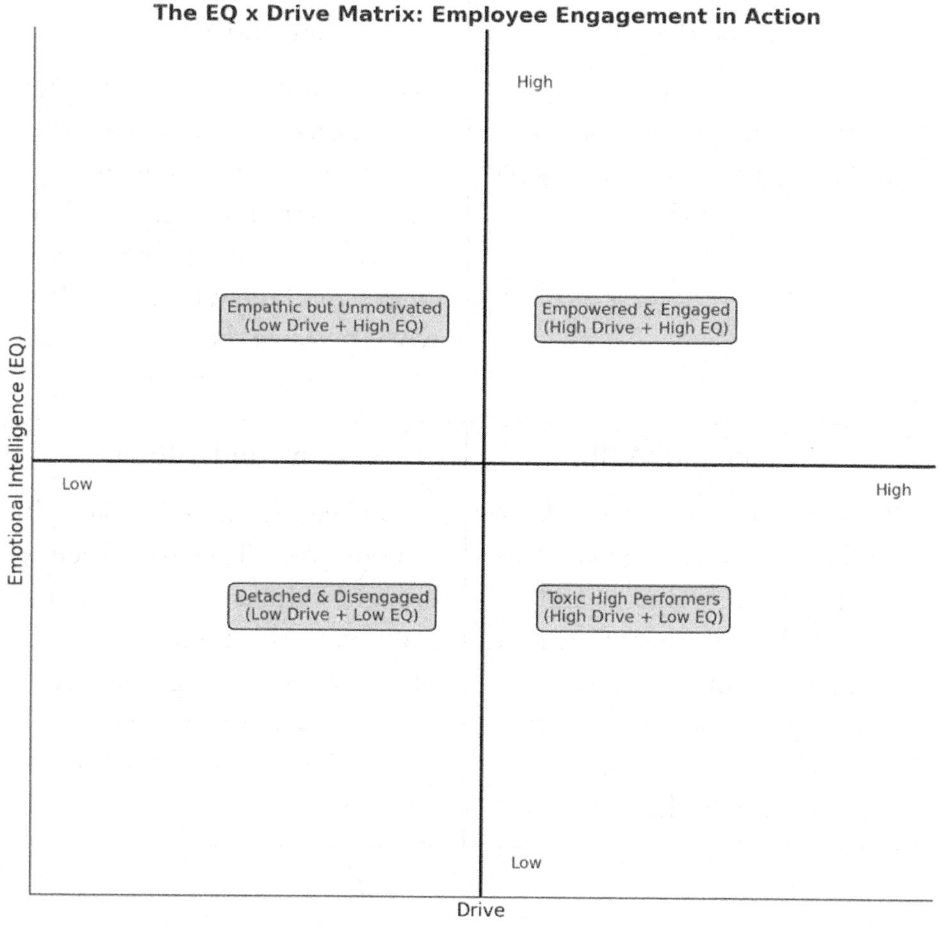

Appendix 8:

Team Evaluation Matrix:

Can and Will These are the employees we want to support and provide autonomy to. Ensure you don't forget them!	**Can and Won't** These employees need to have honest performance conversations, ensure expectations are aligned. They have the skills and need to understand the why, but if they won't perform then this isn't the place for them.
Can't and Will These team members should be trained, provided the necessary tools and resources and provided the support they need to win. This typically is a training gap, or a safety gap- if they don't feel safe enough to ask for help.	**Can't and Won't** Unfortunately, these are typically poor hires. They have been brought in for a role they can not complete, this is ok. But don't keep them too long, support a positive exit while the relationship is still strong.

Appendix 9:

Conversational Courage Matrix

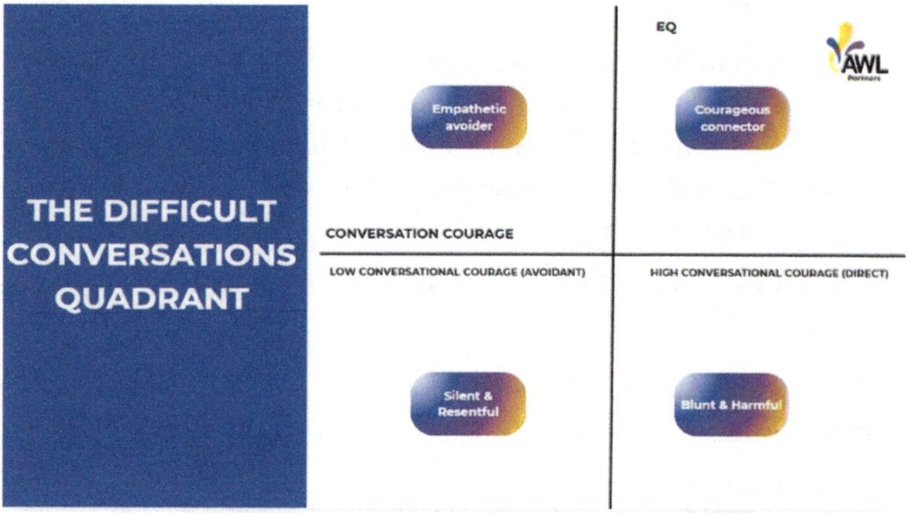

Appendix 10:

People first systems audit:

A practical tool to evaluate whether your processes empower people or exhaust them.

Every system in your organization either adds energy or drains it. This audit helps you assess your processes through a human lens so you can build operational excellence without burning out the people doing the work. Use this audit quarterly, during change, or when team performance starts to dip.

SECTION 1: MENTAL ENERGY: Clarity, Focus & Cognitive Load

Guiding Principle: Systems should reduce mental clutter, not add to it.

Audit Questions:

1. Clarity & Predictability
    - Are workflows easy to understand?
    - Are expectations written down and visible?
    - Do people know "who does what by when"?
2. Cognitive Load
    - Do notifications interrupt deep work?
    - Do tools compete or overlap? (Slack + email + texts + project software)
    - Are we asking people to remember things the system should hold?
3. Autonomy & Efficiency
    - Do people have flexibility to schedule focused work blocks?

- Are tasks sequenced logically?
- Are there unnecessary steps that could be removed?

Rating (Circle One):

Clear & Focused | Needs Adjustment | Overwhelming

Actions to Strengthen Mental Energy:

SECTION 2: EMOTIONAL ENERGY: Trust, Predictability & Psychological Safety

Guiding Principle: Systems must build trust, not trigger fear or uncertainty.

Audit Questions:

1. Communication Expectations
    - Do people know how communication should happen?
    - Are follow-ups defined (what, when, how)?
    - Do processes support clarity or create assumptions?
2. Psychological Safety
    - Do systems make it safe to raise issues early?
    - Are mistakes discussed openly without blame?
    - Are feedback loops built into the workflow?
3. Relational Impact
    - Do processes strengthen relationships or strain them?
    - Is there space for meaningful check-ins?
    - Do leaders model consistent responses?

Rating (Circle One):

Trust-Building | Neutral | Anxiety-Creating

Actions to Strengthen Emotional Energy:

SECTION 3: PHYSICAL ENERGY: Workload, Pace & Operational Flow

Guiding Principle: Systems should support sustainable pace, not perpetual urgency.

Audit Questions:

1. Workload Reality
    - Are workloads aligned with time and capacity?
    - Do systems create unnecessary urgency?
    - Are we tracking the actual time tasks take?
2. Rhythm & Routine
    - Are meetings scheduled with intention?
    - Are breaks, transitions, and recovery time respected?
    - Is there an operating rhythm that prevents burnout?
3. Tools & Ergonomics
    - Do people have what they need to be productive?
    - Are tools designed for speed and ease?
    - Are manual tasks automated where possible?

Rating (Circle One):

Sustainable | Manageable | Draining

Actions to Strengthen Physical Energy:

SECTION 4: SPIRITUAL / PURPOSE ENERGY: **Meaning, Alignment & Contribution**

Guiding Principle: Systems should reinforce the why behind the work and help people feel they matter.

Audit Questions:

1. Pure Alignment
    - Does the system make the purpose of the work visible?
    - Do employees understand how their role creates value?
    - Does the process connect to the customer experience?
2. Values in Action
    - Do systems reflect the organization's real values?
    - Are behaviors rewarded that align with those values?
    - Are there contradictions between "what we say" and "what we do"?
3. Contribution & Recognition
    - Does the system acknowledge wins consistently?
    - Do people feel their efforts are seen?
    - Does the process support growth and development?

Rating (Circle One):

Purpose-Enhancing | Neutral | Purpose-Eroding

Actions to Strengthen Purpose Energy:

FINAL SCORE & ANALYSIS

Summarize the energy systems below into the Red/Yellow/Green Below:

PEOPLE-FIRST SYSTEMS ENERGY MAP

Use this tool to audit how your systems are supporting, or draining, the four core energy systems that drive human performance.

Mental Energy

Clarity ● Focus ● Predictability ● Cognitive Load

Rating: ☐ Green ☐ Yellow ☐ Red

Emotional Energy

Trust ● Safety ● Predictability ● Relationship Flow

Rating: ☐ Green ☐ Yellow ☐ Red

Physical Energy

Workload ● Pace ● Capacity ● Operational Rhythm

Rating: ☐ Green ☐ Yellow ☐ Red

Purpose Energy

Meaning ● Alignment ● Values ● Contribution

Rating: ☐ Green ☐ Yellow ☐ Red

What 1–2 systems need redesign right now?

Who will you involve in the redesign?

RECOMMENDED REDESIGN QUESTIONS

- Use these when planning improvements:
- "What do people actually need here?"
- "Where is energy being wasted?"
- "What decision or step could we remove without losing quality?"
- "Where can we build more clarity?"
- "How can this system strengthen trust?"
- "What would make this feel easier?"
- "What would make this feel meaningful?"

Appendix II:

Everybody Wins Model

Sales as Service: The Everybody Wins Method

When your goal is to serve, not sell – Everybody Wins.

Appendix 12:

Customer Journey Map

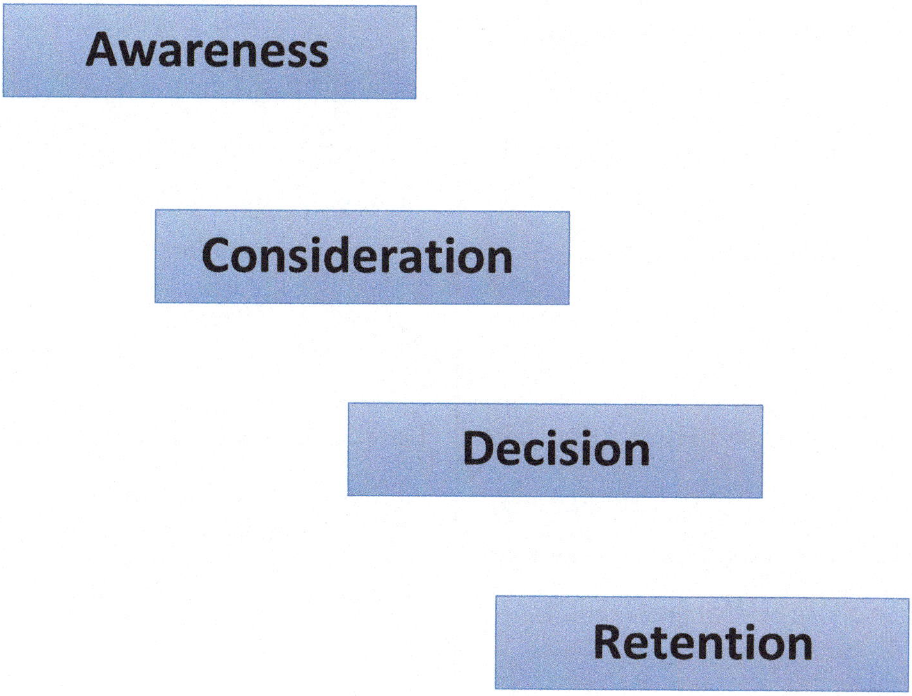

Appendix 13:

The Values-Performance Matrix

High Skill and High Alignment Result: Thrives Leader Focus: Empower and Grow *Shares Values and Performs*	**High Skill and Low Alignment** Result: Friction or flight risk Leader Focus: Clarify values, Coach for alignment *Excellent work but plays by different rules*
Low Skill and High Alignment Result: Growth Opportunity Leader Focus: Train and Develop *Aligned but under skilled*	**Low Skill and Low Alignment** Result: Low trust and low engagement Leader Focus: Compassionate exit *Misfit for role and culture*

Appendix 14:

The Everybody Wins Sales Flow:

References

Achor, S. (2010). *The happiness advantage: The seven principles of positive psychology that fuel success and performance at work.* Crown Business.

Brown, B. (2018). *Dare to lead: Brave work. Tough conversations. Whole hearts.* Random House.

Center for Creative Leadership. (2016). *Empathy in the workplace: A tool for effective leadership.* CCL Press.

Deloitte. (2020). *Global human capital trends: The social enterprise at work.* Deloitte Insights.

Dethmer, J., Chapman, D., & Klemp, K. W. (2015). *The 15 commitments of conscious leadership: A new paradigm for sustainable success.* Conscious Leadership Group.

Edelman. (2024). *Edelman trust barometer.* Edelman Data & Intelligence.

Edmondson, A. C. (2019). *The fearless organization: Creating psychological safety in the workplace for learning, innovation, and growth.* John Wiley & Sons.

Gallup. (2023). *State of the global workplace: 2023 report.* Gallup Press.

Goleman, D. (1995). *Emotional intelligence: Why it can matter more than IQ.* Bantam Books.

Kahneman, D. (2011). *Thinking, fast and slow.* Farrar, Straus and Giroux.

Lencioni, P. (2002). *The five dysfunctions of a team: A leadership fable.* Jossey-Bass.

Pink, D. H. (2009). *Drive: The surprising truth about what motivates us.* Riverhead Books.

Pink, D. H. (2012). *To sell is human: The surprising truth about moving others.* Riverhead Books.

Scott, K. (2017). *Radical candor: Be a kick-ass boss without losing your humanity.* St. Martin's Press.

Scott, S. (2002). *Fierce conversations: Achieving success at work and in life one conversation at a time.* Berkley Books.

Seligman, M. E. P. (2011). *Flourish: A visionary new understanding of happiness and well-being.* Free Press.

Sinek, S. (2009). *Start with why: How great leaders inspire everyone to take action.* Portfolio.

Covey, S. R. (1989). *The 7 habits of highly effective people: Powerful lessons in personal change.* Free Press.

Harvard Business Review. (Various Years). *Leadership and management research articles.* Harvard Business Publishing.

Google. (2016). *Project Aristotle: Understanding team effectiveness.* Google re: Work.

Made in the USA
Monee, IL
03 November 2026

67386759R00134